PROCEEDINGS OF SYMPOSIA IN APPLIED MATHEMATICS

VOLUME 1 NON-LINEAR PROBLEMS IN MECHANICS OF CONTINUA
Edited by E. Reissner (Brown University, August 1947)

VOLUME 2 ELECTROMAGNETIC THEORY
Edited by A. H. Taub (Massachusetts Institute of Technology, July 1948)

VOLUME 3 ELASTICITY
Edited by R. V. Churchill (University of Michigan, June 1949)

VOLUME 4 FLUID DYNAMICS
Edited by M. H. Martin (University of Maryland, June 1951)

VOLUME 5 WAVE MOTION AND VIBRATION THEORY
Edited by A. E. Heins (Carnegie Institute of Technology, June 1952)

VOLUME 6 NUMERICAL ANALYSIS
Edited by J. H. Curtiss (Santa Monica City College, August 1953)

VOLUME 7 APPLIED PROBABILITY
Edited by L. A. MacColl (Polytechnic Institute of Brooklyn, April 1955)

VOLUME 8 CALCULUS OF VARIATIONS AND ITS APPLICATIONS
Edited by L. M. Graves (University of Chicago, April 1956)

VOLUME 9 ORBIT THEORY
Edited by G. Birkhoff and R. E. Langer (New York University, April 1957)

VOLUME 10 COMBINATORIAL ANALYSIS
Edited by R. Bellman and M. Hall, Jr. (Columbia University, April 1958)

VOLUME 11 NUCLEAR REACTOR THEORY
Edited by G. Birkhoff and E. P. Wigner (New York City, April 1959)

VOLUME 12 STRUCTURE OF LANGUAGE AND ITS MATHEMATICAL ASPECTS
Edited by R. Jakobson (New York City, April 1960)

VOLUME 13 HYDRODYNAMIC INSTABILITY
Edited by R. Bellman, G. Birkhoff, C. C. Lin (New York City, April 1960)

VOLUME 14 MATHEMATICAL PROBLEMS IN THE BIOLOGICAL SCIENCES
Edited by R. Bellman (New York City, April 1961)

VOLUME 15 EXPERIMENTAL ARITHMETIC, HIGH SPEED COMPUTING, AND MATHEMATICS
Edited by N. C. Metropolis, A. H. Taub, J. Todd, C. B. Tompkins (Atlantic City and Chicago, April 1962)

VOLUME 16 STOCHASTIC PROCESSES IN MATHEMATICAL PHYSICS AND ENGINEERING
Edited by R. Bellman (New York City, April 1963)

VOLUME 17	APPLICATIONS OF NONLINEAR PARTIAL DIFFERENTIAL EQUATIONS IN MATHEMATICAL PHYSICS *Edited by R. Finn (New York City, April* 1964)
VOLUME 18	MAGNETO-FLUID AND PLASMA DYNAMICS *Edited by H. Grad (New York City, April* 1965)
VOLUME 19	MATHEMATICAL ASPECTS OF COMPUTER SCIENCE *Edited by J. T. Schwartz (New York City, April* 1966)
VOLUME 20	THE INFLUENCE OF COMPUTING ON MATHEMATICAL RESEARCH AND EDUCATION *Edited by J. P. LaSalle (University of Montana, August* 1973)
VOLUME 21	MATHEMATICAL ASPECTS OF PRODUCTION AND DISTRIBUTION OF ENERGY *Edited by P. D. Lax (San Antonio, Texas, January* 1976)
VOLUME 22	NUMERICAL ANALYSIS *Edited by G. H. Golub and J. Oliger (Atlanta, Georgia, January* 1978)
VOLUME 23	MODERN STATISTICS: METHODS AND APPLICATIONS *Edited by R. V. Hogg (San Antonio, Texas, January* 1980)
VOLUME 24	GAME THEORY AND ITS APPLICATIONS *Edited by W. F. Lucas (Biloxi, Mississippi, January* 1979)
VOLUME 25	OPERATIONS RESEARCH: MATHEMATICS AND MODELS *Edited by S. I. Gass (Duluth, Minnesota, August* 1979)
VOLUME 26	THE MATHEMATICS OF NETWORKS *Edited by S. A. Burr (Pittsburgh, Pennsylvania, August* 1981)
VOLUME 27	COMPUTED TOMOGRAPHY *Edited by L. A. Shepp (Cincinnati, Ohio, January* 1982)
VOLUME 28	STATISTICAL DATA ANALYSIS *Edited by R. Gnanadesikan (Toronto, Ontario, August* 1982)

AMS SHORT COURSE LECTURE NOTES
published as a subseries of
Proceedings of Symposia in Applied Mathematics

APPLIED CRYPTOLOGY, CRYPTOGRAPHIC PROTOCOLS, and COMPUTER SECURITY MODELS

PROCEEDINGS OF SYMPOSIA
IN APPLIED MATHEMATICS
Volume 29

APPLIED CRYPTOLOGY, CRYPTOGRAPHIC PROTOCOLS, and COMPUTER SECURITY MODELS

AMERICAN MATHEMATICAL SOCIETY
PROVIDENCE, RHODE ISLAND

LECTURE NOTES PREPARED FOR THE
AMERICAN MATHEMATICAL SOCIETY SHORT COURSE

CRYPTOLOGY IN REVOLUTION: MATHEMATICS AND MODELS

HELD IN SAN FRANCISCO, CALIFORNIA
JANUARY 5–6, 1981

By
Richard A. DeMillo
George I. Davida
David P. Dobkin
Michael A. Harrison
Richard J. Lipton

The AMS Short Course Series is sponsored by the Society's Committee on Employment and Education Policy (CEEP). The series is under the direction of the Short Course Advisory Subcommittee of CEEP.

Library of Congress Cataloging in Publication Data

Main entry under title:
Applied cryptology, cryptographic protocols, and computer security models.
(Proceedings of symposia in applied mathematics, ISSN 0160-7634; v. 29. AMS short course lecture notes)
Expanded version of notes prepared for the AMS short course entitled Cryptology in revolution, mathematics and models, held in San Francisco, Calif., Jan. 5–6, 1981, by Richard A. DeMillo and others.
Bibliography: p.
1. Computers–Access control. 2. Cryptography. I. DeMillo, Richard A. II. American Mathematical Society. III. Series: Proceedings of symposia in applied mathematics; v. 29. IV. Series: Proceedings of symposia in applied mathematics; v. 29. AMS short course lecture notes.
QA76.9.A25A66 1983 001.64 83-15548
ISBN 0-8218-0041-8

1980 Mathematics Subject Classification. Primary 68-02, 68B99, 68C99.

This volume was printed directly from copy prepared by the authors.

Contents

Preface

On January 5-6, 1981, the authors delivered a series of lectures entitled 'Cryptology in Revolution: Mathematics and Models' to a meeting of the American Mathematical Society. This survey of cryptology and computer security is an edited and expanded version of the notes which AMS published for the original lecture series.

The presentation is organized as follows. A survey of cryptographic theory which emphasizes the two major developments of contemporary cryptography (the federal data encryption standard and public-key cryptography) is presented in Chapter 2. Chapter 3 presents a survey of the security problems which arise in the use of time-shared and networked digital computers. Finally a number of protocols which are used to achieve levels of security in computer sytems and the emerging theory surrounding cryptographic protocols are presented in Chapter 4. As this survey is being compiled, some friction exists between certain U.S. Government agencies, academic researchers, and professional societies. A brief account of the issues which have led to this controvery is given in Chapter 1.

This work was supported in part by the National Science Foundation, under grants MCS79-03428, MCS81-03608, and MCS-08012716 and the Office of Naval research under contracts N00014-79-C-0231 and N00014-79-C-0873.

1. Introduction

We use the term computer system to describe collections of computational resources. These resources may communicate with each other or may comprise independent computers that interact only with human programmers and operators. With increasing frequency, computer systems are relied upon in applications where the successful completion of tasks and activities is especially critical. In many cases, a computer system is required to function without error or within certain efficiency bounds. The extent to which the systems fulfills such requirements is used to define the _reliability_ or _performance_ of the system. In highly reliable or efficient systems, system behavior is measured against its response to external input which lies within a certain range that has been _specified_ as acceptable. Input lying outside the specified range may cause the system to fail or to become inefficient, but, since the system meets its requirements on the input for which it was designed, its reliability or level of performance are not affected by such input.

There are applications, however, for which such notions as reliability are unsuitable. In these applications, the range of specified input is determined by an adversary or _enemy_ whose goals is to subvert the successful functioning of the system. Thus, although input from the enemy may be outside the normal operating range, the system must continue to provide essential services, _in spite of_ the input. For example, military or diplomatic communication systems must continue to deliver messages in a highly regular and predictable way, even though enemies may attempt to intercept secret communications, corrupt messages, or insert false messages into the system. Another example of a system whose successful operation requires withstanding subversion is an electronic funds transfer system. Such a system must protect financial transactions against intentional or unintentional disruption and diversion. By the same token, large scale databases of electronically stored information may contain data that is sensitive. Such data may be composed of financial records, personal data, or proprietary information. Such databases must deliver access and services without compromising the sensitive data.

The _security_ of a computer system is defined by its ability to meet specific operating requirements, despite the actions of a knowledgeable and determined enemy. Security requirements may include maintaining the secrecy or integrity of information, providing highly reliable or available services, or preventing unauthorized use of system resources.

In this survey of, we will concentrate on three important aspects of system security: cryptography, software approaches, and cryptographic protocols.

Cryptography is the art of concealing the content of messages from an enemy who may be monitoring system activity. The rapid spread of communication-based technology and the recent appearance of cryptographic techniques that provide highly secure message concealment, have led to a renewed interest in the field of cryptography. However, many of the security problems which arise from the use of modern computing technology cannot be <u>directly</u> solved by cryptographic techniques.

An alternative approach to solving security problems is to <u>program</u> the computer to monitor or protect against the most probable threats. Two important areas are the protection mechanisms which guard against unauthorized access or dangerous program execution and the protection of information stored in statistical databases. There are situations, however, in which software-oriented approaches to security must be augmented by still more secure system components. It is possible that by executing a cryptographic <u>protocol</u>, that is, an exchange of secret messages, more complex security mechanisms can be implemented.

The format of this survey is as follows. Chapter 2 will discuss data security, paying particular attention to modern techniques of encryption and cryptanalysis. In Chapter 3, we present the technical basis of access control modelling and multilevel system requirements and highlight the most useful models for multilevel security. The emphasis in Chapter 4 is on an alternative view of how security requirements can be met: through the use of protocols built on highly secure cryptographic techniques.

It will be clear as we proceed that this is not an unbiased survey, and the reader should beware that for every opinion offered herein, there is ample contrary argument available in other technical circles. In the United States, for example, support has been consistent and sizable for other approaches to the multilevel problem. These approaches have, however, not met with great practical success. We hope that these views are accepted as alternatives to competing positions. We certainly do not offer them as replacements. Quite the contrary: we have not seen the alternative views discussed with any depth.

It is an interesting footnote to the technical developments discussed in the sequel that the noticeable increase in academic research activity in the area of computer security has lead to confrontations with agencies of the U.S. Government. On one hand, agencies such as the National Security Agency (NSA) have issued claims that their missions may be imperiled by the publication of certain results in cryptography. Some researchers have countered, on the other hand, that any restriction on the flow of research results constitutes an uneccessary and serious infringement of academic and intellectual freedom. They argue further that the stuff of basic research in cryptography is pure mathematics and computer science; it is not clear how to distinguish a pure number theoretic or complexity theoretic result from one which poses a genuine threat to national security. The alternative of restricting all basic research which which impinges on sensitive applications is probably not workable.

In 1980, the American Council on Education (ACE) formed a panel to study the issues raised by the differing viewpoints noted above. The ACE group ultimately recommended a system of voluntary reviews by NSA. The ACE recommendations contain the assumption that without compulsory pressures, most authors and professional societies will cooperate with such a system of voluntary review. One of us (Davida) was a member of the ACE study group, and did not concur with their recommendations. In a minority statement, it was argued that any system of restraint -- even one which is voluntary -- will only hinder the development of cryptography in public and private sectors, to the ultimate detriment of the public and NSA itself. Two of us (DeMillo and Lipton) served on a panel of representatives from the professional societies to outline a response to proposed regulation of cryptographic research. As yet, there is no definitive resolution to the underlying problems.*

---

*The complete text of the ACE study group report has been published under the tile 'Report of the Public Cryptography Study Group' in the Communications of the ACM, 24(7): 434-449.

2. Cryptography

When messages can be protected from disclosure by physical means, no interesting theoretical problems arise -- security rests on the effectiveness of physical barriers. An intriguing problem does arise, however, when a message must be securely communicated to a friendly recipient. The term 'communication' is to be taken in its most general sense. Figure 2.1 shows an idealized communications environment.

Figure 2.1
Generalized Communications Environment

The communications medium may be a slip of paper on which a message is written, an information-theoretic channel, or a physical file on a computer system. The security problem in such a setting is to 'write' the message in such a way that an enemy, even if he eavesdrops on the communications medium, cannot deduce the contents of the message.

The problem of secret writing is a very old one, and the many attempts to secure sensitive messages (particularly military and diplomatic messages) have endowed the field with a rich history and a devoted following of amateur and professional experts (see the bibliographic notes at the end of this section). The use of these techniques in computer systems has given rise to a new and increasingly sophisticated technology, and it is on these applications that we will concentrate.

2.1 Ciphers and Cryptosystems. To guarantee the security of messages placed in the communications medium, the system shown in Figure 2.1 is endowed with additional structure -- it becomes a _cryptosystem_. In a cryptosystem there is an _enemy_ or attacker who has access to the communications medium. The enemy is also assumed to have computational resources and memory at his disposal. Like the noisy channel of information theory, the enemy may introduce errors into messages he sees in the medium. Unlike a noisy channel, however, the enemy does not always corrupt messages with random errors; he may introduce highly biased errors to confuse or deceive the receiver. The enemy may have three -- not always exclusive -- goals in affecting normal communications:

1. violating the secrecy of the communication,
2. confounding the receiver with a corrupted message,
3. deceiving either the transmitter or the receiver or both about the identity of the opposite party.

The first threat, violating the privacy of the transmitter, is the most familiar incarnation of the cryptographic problem. Protecting the communication in the presence of an enemy who pursues the latter goals are problems which have come into prominance only recently. These are problems of _integrity_ and _authentication_, respectively. For example, the authentication problem arises in the login procedure for multiuser computer systems when the system software (the receiver) must insure that the login name it receives belongs to a legitimate user (a transmitter) and not to an intruder attempting to illegally use the computer. The integrity problem arises in electronic funds transfer (EFT) systems: a corruption of a funds transfer could result in funds being deposited in an unauthorized account belonging to the enemy.

These threats can be met by exploiting the most notable characteristic of a cryptosystem; the transmitter does not place the message itself in the communications medium. Rather, a second message is transmitted, a message _related_ to the original message by a transformation known to the the transmitter and by a (possibly different) transformation known to the receiver. The difficulty of unraveling this relationship without exact knowledge of the transformations is what gives various cryptosystems their specialized properties. Figure 2.2 shows an idealized cryptosystem.

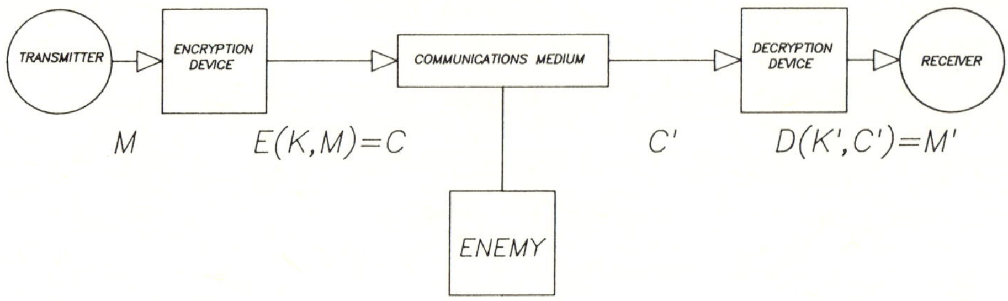

Figure 2.2
A Cryptosystem for Transmitting Message M

The transmitter composes a message M (the plaintext) and submits M to an encryption or enciphering device. The encryption device invokes an encrypting function E. The enciphering transformation is determined by two parameters. In addition to the plaintext, M, E also requires some additional information, K, called the encrypting key. In this sense, E determines a class of message transformations E_K such that $E_K(M) = E(K,M)$ whenever K is a valid key and M is a valid message. From the point of view of an observer who does not have access to an encrypting key, a good E will spread the plaintext messages evenly and apparently randomly over a set of messages called the ciphertext. The encrypting key may be held by the transmitter, by the device or by a third party. The ciphertext C is placed onto the communications medium where the enemy may examine it, store it, operate on it, and, finally, corrupt it to C'. The decryption device invokes a decrypting algorithm D. D takes two arguments: the alleged ciphertext C' and a decrypting key, K'. The nature of K' is fixed by the nature of the cryptosystem, but in general, K' depends on K (in a conventional cipher, K=K') in such a way that $\{D_{K'}\}$ determines a class of algorithms for which

$$E_K(M) = C \text{ implies } D_{K'}(C) = M.$$

That is, K' represents the minimal amount of information that the decrypting device needs in order to recover plaintext from ciphertext. In Figure 2.2, the ciphertext may have been corrupted by the enemy so that $M' \neq M$. The threats that must be met are:

Threat to Secrecy: M = M' and the enemy is able to determine M from C and possibly other information.

Threat to Integrity: $M \neq M'$ but neither the transmitter nor the receiver is able to detect the corruption of C.

Threat to Authorization: C' is composed by the enemy, but the receiver believes that C' is ciphertext originating from the transmitter.

As we will discuss in a later section, it is possible to respond to authorization and integrity threats by responding to secrecy threats only and using protocols , i.e., algorithms known to all participants in a cryptographic exchange) to insure that the enemy cannot corrupt the message or impersonate the transmitter. Threats to secrecy cannot be met simply by insuring that $E_K = D_{K'}^{-1}$ -- that condition is trivially satisfied by the identity transformation which provides no secrecy whatsoever! It must be the case that the enemy cannot infer M from C. The process of deriving a general solution to such an inference problem (e.g., an algorithm to derive K' from samples of C) is known as cryptanalysis. What is the meaning of 'cannot infer'? Obviously, practical requirements vary from the strict security requirements placed on many military systems to the rather bland security requirements of some commercial applications. One view to which we will return later is that the communications medium together with the enemy constitutes a game-theoretic channel and the purpose of the cryptosystem is to make a winning strategy for the channel as unlikely as possible.

There are essentially only two possibilities for constructing the encrypting/decrypting devices: codes and ciphers. A code uses the entire plaintext language as a basis for constructing C;, that is, the code must have established the semantic content of every possible message to be sent through the system. The only way to encode messages through such a system is to provide a code-book, a list of possible messages and their encoded values, to the transmitter and to the receiver. Since there need be no relationship at all between the plaintext phrases and the ciphertext of the code-book (other than the completely arbitrary one established by the code-book itself) there is very little of theoretical significance that can be said about this approach. The problem with codes is that unless the phrase to be transmitted has already been conceived and placed in the code-book, communication is not possible. A cipher, on the other hand, exploits only the symbolic nature of the transmission; a cipher is a mapping that assigns new symbols of ciphertext to symbols or groups of symbols in the plaintext. Since every message is composed of plaintext symbols and the cipher completely specifies how plaintext symbols are to be replaced by ciphertext symbols, communication of arbitrary messages is possible.

There is a problem raised by ciphers: the relationship between ciphertext and plaintext is no longer the arbitrary one imposed by a code-book, rather, it is an extension of the simpler relationship between symbols in ciphertext and plaintext and so may be revealed by cryptanalysis.

For the purposes of this survey, we will distinguish between ciphers which carry out the encipherment by alphabetic substitutions, that is, which treat the plain text as a sequence of symbols to be encrypted (these ciphers are called _stream_ ciphers) and ciphers which divide messages into blocks of characters of fixed length -- possibly after padding or compressing the message -- and derive ciphertext from plaintext by operating on blocks of characters rather than streams of characters (these ciphers are called _block_ ciphers). Although stream ciphers retain their importance for many applications, it is block ciphers which have had the greatest recent impact on the field of cryptography. Modern computers naturally group alphabetic characters into strings of binary digits, so block encipherment can be viewed as an arithmetic problem and the security properties of the encrypting algorithms can be treated analytically. Moreover, by permitting substitutions on large blocks of plaintext at hardware speeds, very high speed encrypted data transmission can take place.

Categorizing ciphers into stream and block ciphers has another advantage. In a stream cipher, the basic allowable operation on a message is the _substitution_ of one symbol for another. That is, if the message M to be transmitted is composed of symbols from an alphabet A,

$$M = a_1 \ldots a_n, \text{ each } a_i \in A,$$

then C must be defined with respect to n substituions $f_1, \ldots, f_n$ on A. In other words,

$$C = f_1(a_1) f_2(a_2) \ldots f_n(a_n),$$

each $f_i : A \dashrightarrow A$, $a_i \in A$. It is possible that each f_i also depends on one or more predecessors. With a block cipher, the concept of substitution still makes sense, but now there is an additional operation that can be defined: <u>permutation</u>. Suppose that the message M is composed of m blocks $B_1 \ldots B_m$ of n characters each. Then

$$C = C_1 \ldots C_m,$$

but now for each i, $1 \leq i \leq m$, if

$$B_i = b_1 \ldots b_n, \text{ each } b_j \in A,$$

then

$$C_i = b_{\pi(1)} \ldots b_{\pi(n)},$$

where π is a permutation of the integers $1, \ldots, n$. Thus a block cipher can be viewed as composed from a <u>network</u> of components which successively substitute for elements of A and permute positions within a block of characters. Figure 2.3 shows such a network (called an S/P network):

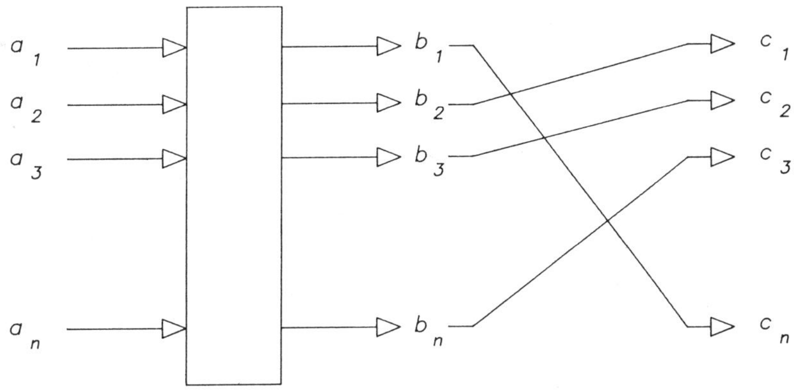

Figure 2.3
One Stage of a Substitution-Permutation (S/P) Network

2.2 Stream Ciphers. From now on, we will systematically confuse letters of the alphabet a,b,c, ... with their position in the usual ordering of the alphabet. Marks of punctuation and the digits are not directly represented in this way, but all of the following extends to a more realistic alphabet in an entirely straightforward way.

Legend assigns Julius Caesar credit for suggesting the following stream cipher:

$$f(x) = x+3 \pmod{26}.$$

Any cipher which is expressible by

$$f(x) = x+K \pmod{26}$$

is called a <u>Vigenere</u> cipher. Figure 2.4 shows the so-called Vigenere square -- a complete description of all possible Vigenere ciphers.

Plain--->	A	B	C	D	E	F	G	H	I	J	K	L	M	N	O	P	Q	R	S	T	U	V	W	X	Y	Z
Cipher	a	b	c	d	e	f	g	h	i	j	k	l	m	n	o	p	q	r	s	t	u	v	w	x	y	z
|	b	c	d	e	f	g	h	i	j	k	l	m	n	o	p	q	r	s	t	u	v	w	x	y	z	a
|	c	d	e	f	g	h	i	j	k	l	m	n	o	p	q	r	s	t	u	v	w	x	y	z	a	b
V	d	e	f	g	h	i	j	k	l	m	n	o	p	q	r	s	t	u	v	w	x	y	z	a	b	c
	e	f	g	h	i	j	k	l	m	n	o	p	q	r	s	t	u	v	w	x	y	z	a	b	c	d
	f	g	h	i	j	k	l	m	n	o	p	q	r	s	t	u	v	w	x	y	z	a	b	c	d	e
	g	h	i	j	k	l	m	n	o	p	q	r	s	t	u	v	w	x	y	z	a	b	c	d	e	f
	h	i	j	k	l	m	n	o	p	q	r	s	t	u	v	w	x	y	z	a	b	c	d	e	f	g
	i	j	k	l	m	n	o	p	q	r	s	t	u	v	w	x	y	z	a	b	c	d	e	f	g	h
	j	k	l	m	n	o	p	q	r	s	t	u	v	w	x	y	z	a	b	c	d	e	f	g	h	i
	k	l	m	n	o	p	q	r	s	t	u	v	w	x	y	z	a	b	c	d	e	f	g	h	i	j
	l	m	n	o	p	q	r	s	t	u	v	w	x	y	z	a	b	c	d	e	f	g	h	i	j	k
	m	n	o	p	q	r	s	t	u	v	w	x	y	z	a	b	c	d	e	f	g	h	i	j	k	l
	n	o	p	q	r	s	t	u	v	w	x	y	z	a	b	c	d	e	f	g	h	i	j	k	l	m
	o	p	q	r	s	t	u	v	w	x	y	z	a	b	c	d	e	f	g	h	i	j	k	l	m	n
	p	q	r	s	t	u	v	w	x	y	z	a	b	c	d	e	f	g	h	i	j	k	l	m	n	o
	q	r	s	t	u	v	w	x	y	z	a	b	c	d	e	f	g	h	i	j	k	l	m	n	o	p
	r	s	t	u	v	w	x	y	z	a	b	c	d	e	f	g	h	i	j	k	l	m	n	o	p	q
	s	t	u	v	w	x	y	z	a	b	c	d	e	f	g	h	i	j	k	l	m	n	o	p	q	r
	t	u	v	w	x	y	z	a	b	c	d	e	f	g	h	i	j	k	l	m	n	o	p	q	r	s
	u	v	w	x	y	z	a	b	c	d	e	f	g	h	i	j	k	l	m	n	o	p	q	r	s	t
	v	w	x	y	z	a	b	c	d	e	f	g	h	i	j	k	l	m	n	o	p	q	r	s	t	u
	w	x	y	z	a	b	c	d	e	f	g	h	i	j	k	l	m	n	o	p	q	r	s	t	u	v
	x	y	z	a	b	c	d	e	f	g	h	i	j	k	l	m	n	o	p	q	r	s	t	u	v	w
	y	z	a	b	c	d	e	f	g	h	i	j	k	l	m	n	o	p	q	r	s	t	u	v	w	x
	z	a	b	c	d	e	f	g	h	i	j	k	l	m	n	o	p	q	r	s	t	u	v	w	x	y

Figure 2.4
The Vigenere Alphabets

Each substitution alphabet is uniquely identified by both the amount of shift K and by its starting letter. Thus, there are only 26 keys for a cryptosystem built on such a cipher. It is easy to see how successful cryptanalysis of such a system would work, even if the enemy knows nothing about the message. Upon receipt of cipher text C, the enemy simply chooses a string of characters long enough to contain a meaningful message fragment. The enemy then carries out all possible substitutions on the reduced piece of ciphertext until he finds a meaningful translation. Solving the cipher is then equivalent to solving a linear congruence.

Thus, the major difficulty with Vigenere ciphers is that the cryptanalyst can count on the ordering of the ciphertext characters to be the same as in the alphabet A. The process of destroying this ordering information is known as <u>decimation</u> of an alphabetic sequence. If a and n are integers with $(a,n)=1$, then the residues $a, 2a, \ldots, na$ modulo n are all distinct. Thus, a cipher which destroys the normal alphabetic order is

$$f(x) = ax \pmod{26},$$

where a is relatively prime to 26. The constant a is known as the decimation interval. Once the sequence has been decimated it is, of course, possible to shift by an amount b (mod 26), so that a general decimating cipher is given by the linear transformation

$$g(x) = ax + b \pmod{26}.$$

To use g in a cryptosystem, the transmitter and receiver share the key (a,b). To encrypt, the transmitter computes for every symbol y, $g(y)=c$. To decrypt, the receiver solves the congruence

$$c = ax + b \pmod{26}.$$

If a and b are relatively prime, the congruence is uniquely solvable for x. This technique would appear to provide increased security. For example, comparing decimated alphabetic symbol frequencies for ciphertext and standard messages is not such an easy job, because the decimation has changed the shape of the frequency distribution. Still, if the enemy can determine two cipher-plaintext pairs (c_1,x_1) and (c_2,x_2), he can solve the congruences

$$c_1 = ax_1 + b \pmod{26}$$

$$c_2 = ax_2 + b \pmod{26}$$

for the decimation interval a and the shift amount b. This is the general line of attack for decimations based on linear transformations. One way of obtaining such ciphertext-plaintext pairs is to to examine the ciphertext for low frequency digraphs (symbol pairs) and high frequency *digraphs*. Since the plaintext alphabet separation of digraphs is known, the cryptanalyst can guess decimation intervals and plaintext-ciphertext pairs.

Thus, linear transformations have an inherent weakness: knowledge of cipher-plaintext pairs reveals too much about the substitution. This difficulty is apparently avoided if there is a *random* assignment of ciphertext letters to plaintext letters. However, the very randomness of the assignment means that the size of the key must be the size of the complete alphabetic sequence. Therefore, most cryptographic problems based on random assignment try to systematically induce a random-looking assignment. While these ciphers make entertaining puzzles, they also fall to frequency approaches -- usually by tables of suffixes and prefixes, distinguishing vowels from consonants, looking for 'pattern words', counting digraphs and trigraphs, and working on short (five letter) cipher fragments.

The encryption schemes above always encipher into a single fixed cipher alphabet. In such schemes, encipherment is said to be *monoalphabetic*. The usual method of attack on a monoalphabetic system is to use the fact that certain statistical properties of the plaintext alphabet are carried over into the cipher alphabet -- solution of the cipher is possible because a plaintext letter is *always* represented by the same ciphertext letter. An additional factor of confusion might, therefore, be added by using several cipher alphabets. For example, a key may be a sequence of designations of Vigenere alphabets. Even occurrences of digraphs can apparently be obliterated by these substitutions. Such ciphers are known as *polyalphabetic* ciphers, and most of conventional cryptanalytic theory is based on their solution.

The apparent security of complex polyalphabetic ciphers forms the basis for *rotor machines*. Very simply, the rotor machines determine, by mechanical gears and electrical interconnections of typewriter keys to indicator lights, a sequence of substitution alphabets. For example, the military version of the German Enigma determines a substitution alphabet by interactions of several substitutions. First, a plugboard substitution P results in a systematic interchange of letters. This substitution is self-reciprocal in the sense that that $P^{-1} = P$. A series of rewirings of keyboard to input lines results in a substitution E. Next, a series of enciphering rotors each determines a substitution. The rotors also determine the subsequent substitutions. If Q represents a rotor substitution at some position, then the other rotated positions are generated by the group of substitutions

$$C^{-i}QC^{i},$$

where C^i is the cipher x+i(mod 26). A final rotor, the reflector, yields a substitution based on 13 interchanges of alphabetic characters. A plaintext character x may then be enciphered by:

$$P^{-1}E^{-1}R_1{}^{-1}R_2{}^{-1}R_3{}^{-1}RR_3R_2\ R_1EP(x) = c.$$

The procedure for encipherment requires a daily setting of plugs and rotors. A message begins with a 'telegram key' of three letters, whose encipherment by the receiving machine determines the final setting of the three enciphering rotors to be used for the transmission. If E=I (as, in fact, was the case in the military version of Enigma) and the total rotor state is represented by Z, then a solution is represented by rewriting the equation above as

$$P^{-1}Z_iP(x_i) = c_i$$

for each of the rotor positions Z_i for the known plaintext $x_1,\ldots,x_n$. Since P is self-reciprocal, this reduces to

$$Z_iP(x_i) = P(c_i).$$

By careful analysis of the consistency of given data with the assumption of the existence of the required P, it is possible in principle to test a rotor position and its subsequent positions by mechanical means, but the number of possibilities to be tried grows combinatorially. However, it is possible to mechanically solve Enigma by careful pruning of the branching tree of possible P's to be tried. It is an interesting historical note that in the World War II cryptanalysis of Enigma, the transmitters made it easy to obtain plaintext to use in the cryptanalysis. Common telegram keys were AAA, BBB, CCC, and so on. Even when it was required that such keys not be used, this information was known to the cryptanalysts. Futhermore, several transmitters were prone to sending such stylized messages that the analysts could guess plaintext.

Although the amount of computation needed to cryptanalyze

polyalphabetic ciphers can be quite forbidding, they are not secure. As the Enigma example shows, the application of knowledge concerning plaintext messages, the design of E, and general properties of sets of substitutions can be combined with massive calculations to exhaustively search out solutions to such systems. There is a notable exception, however.

When the key length is permitted to be as long as the message itself, a perfectly secure stream cipher can be constructed. A variation on the Vigenere cipher, called the _Vernam cipher_, or the _one-time pad_, is constructed as follows. Let M be the message $a_1 \ldots a_n$, where each a_i is expressed as a binary digit 0,1. A key for M is a sequence of binary digits $K = k_1 \ldots k_n$. Encipherment is obtained by the bitwise addition of messages and key modulo 2 (denoted $\oplus$). Thus, to encipher M, the transmitter forms

$$M \oplus K = C,$$

while the receiver decrypts by calculating

$$C \oplus K = M.$$

If the key is random, the cipher is theoretically unbreakable (see Section 2.3). To use such a cryptosystem, the correspondents must each have in their possession identical random 'key tapes' from which the 'next' n bits can be extracted to form the key for the current message. This may result in unacceptable amounts of key information to be exchanged, so it is natural to ask whether the key distribution requirements can be reduced in some fashion. For example, can a short random key be used over and over? The answer is no, not with absolute security, since the resulting periodicity can be exploited by a cryptanalyst. A variation on this idea is to use the ⊕ of two small keys of length n_1 and n_2, where $(n_1,n_2)=1$. The period of the resulting key is n_1n_2. Even this scheme has been successfully cryptanalyzed.

2.3 Information-Theoretic Cryptanalysis. A cryptographic key represents information about which the enemy is ignorant. Due to the nature of a cryptosystem it is not possible to assume that the enemy does not know the nature of the cryptographic algorithm in use. In addition to the algorithm, the enemy may also have access to other information which can be of use in analyzing a cipher.

<u>Ciphertext Only Analysis</u>: In this attack on the system, the enemy only has access to the ciphertext he sees on the medium. Although it is a very weak sort of attack, there are many ciphertext only analyses available of apparently secure ciphers. Most ciphertext only attacks work through frequency counts and statistical properties of language.

<u>Known Plaintext Analysis</u>: The enemy in a known plaintext attack has several plaintext-ciphertext pairs from which to work. The example of the Enigma analysis shows how this information can be used to analyze the system. The Enigma example also shows that it is easy enough to gain probable plaintext -- a cryptographic system which cannot withstand a known plaintext assault cannot be considered secure.

<u>Chosen Plaintext Analysis</u>: In a chosen plaintext analysis, the enemy can submit unlimited portions of plaintext to the system and observe the corresponding ciphertext. It is obviously the most severe attack that can be mounted on a cryptosystem.

In assessing the security of any system, we usually assume the worst case. For cryptosystems, the worst case is that the enemy is attempting a chosen plaintext analysis of the system and has access to all system information _except_ the cryptographic key. There are two ways to assess the security of a system. First, a system can be called secure if it is _unconditionally_ secure, that is, if the enemy, regardless of the computational power he brings to bear on the problem, cannot analyze the system. That sounds very much like a worst case analysis, but it may, in fact, be too pessimistic. If the result of an unconditional security requirement is that no usable system is secure, then either the idea of security has to be abandoned or the worst case capabilities of the enemy must be more carefully assessed. If, for example, the enemy can only successfully cryptanalyze the system with an impossibly powerful computer, then an unconditionally insecure system may, in practice, be perfectly secure.

In this section, we will sketch the information-theoretic model of security. In the next section, we present a model based on _feasible_ attacks by the enemy. The distinction between the concepts is crucial and has lead to the current advances in cryptographic theory.

The theory of unconditional security parallels the information theory of noisy channels. Let the encryption algorithm be $E(.,.)$ as described above. If message M is enciphered as $E(K,M)=C$, then the enemy observing the communications medium will attempt to obtain M from C by applying a cryptanalytic function h; in general, $h(C) = M' \neq M$ -- notice that h is not a function of the key K' since knowledge of K' is concealed from the enemy. E is <u>secure</u> if it is not possible that $h(C) = M$, regardless of how h is chosen. In other words, it seems reasonable to regard the cryptosystem as secure if

$$\mathrm{Prob}\{h(C)=M\} < \varepsilon.$$

It is usual to assume that each message occurs with probability $P(M)$ and that each potential ciphertext C will fall into the enemy's hands with probability $P(C)$. Let **K** be the set of available keys. Keys are chosen randomly and uniformly from **K**. If $E_K(M) = C$ for all $K \in \mathbf{K}$, then the conditional probability of C given that a key in **K** is used for encipherment is denoted $P_M(C)$ (cf. the known-plaintext attack described above). Then E is unconditionally secure if $P_M(C)$ is independent of M:

$$P_M(C) = P(C).$$

In information theoretic terms, the uncertainty of the keys should be at least as great as the uncertainty of the messages.

Suppose that X is the transmitter of a stream of bits to Y in the presence of an enemy Z. If the communications medium is a <u>binary symmetric channel</u>, then Z will see $u \oplus 1$ with probability p, if u is the bit actually sent by X. If the channel is simply noisy, then Z <u>is</u> the receiver, and the corruption of u with probability p is due to the channel. If Z is the enemy, then the 'corruption' is really the result of encipherment. In either case, I -- the uncertainty <u>removed</u> -- is defined by

$$I = \sum\sum p(x,z)\ [\log(p(z|x)/p(z))],$$

where the summations are over the messages x,z sent and received by X and Z.

In applying information theory to noisy channel coding, the point is to maximize I. In cryptology, we would like to have I = 0. In this simple cryptosystem this condition obtains when p=0.5. Thus, in this model, the perfect concealer of messages is the Vernam cipher:

$$C = M \oplus K.$$

When Prob{K=1} = Prob{K=0} = 0.5,

$$\text{Prob}\{h(c_1 \ldots c_k) = m_1 \ldots m_k\} \leq 2^{-k}.$$

It is usually more convenient to work with the related measures of <u>entropy</u> and <u>equivocation</u>. If I is the uncertainty removed, then -I is the equivocation, the average ambiguity in the transmission.

More generally, assume that all messages of exactly N symbols chosen from a fixed alphabet A, $|A| = L$, so that there are L^N possible messages. The quantity $R_0 = \log(L)$ is sometimes called the <u>absolute rate</u> of the language, and so the number of possible messages is also given by

$$L^N = 2^{R_0 N},$$

and, assuming that the ciphertext is also written in A, this also expresses the number of possible ciphertexts. From the point of view of the transmitter, some messages are meaningful and so occur with nonzero probability, while some messages are meaningless, and, assuming a rational transmitter, occur with probability zero. The number of meaningful messages is assumed to be 2^{RN}, where the quantity R is called the <u>rate</u> of the language. Each meaningful message occurs with probability 2^{-RN}. The redundancy of a language is a measure of the number of different expressions for a given meaningful message: formally, the redundancy D is

$$D = R_0 - R.$$

The number of keys is defined to be 2^H, where each key is equally likely. The constant H is called the key entropy. The point of a cryptosystem is to create doubt on the part of the enemy as to the exact nature of the message M. As in the case of the binary symmetric channel, the only information to which the enemy does not have access is the key, so the entropy of a random key should represent the amount of uncertainty of the enemy given that he has received C. The equivocation introduced is the uncertainty introduced in the system by hiding the key. There are two sorts of equivocation which are important in determining the security of the system. Suppose that the message M_1 is enciphered to $E(K_1,M_1) = C_1$ by the key K_1. If there is no other meaningful message M so that $D(K,C_1) = M$, then -- remember that the enemy has arbitrary resources at his disposal -- it must be assumed that the enemy will eventually discover this fact and so compromise C_1. If, on the other hand. $E(K_2,M_2) = C_1$, where M_2 is also meaningful, then the enemy cannot compromise C_1 since it legally and meaningfully decrypts ambiguously (e.g. in the binary symmetric channel I = 0). Let N(m) be a random variable which represents the number of meaningful messages which encrypt to C. If, for a suitably large constant Q,

$$\mathrm{Prob}\{N(m) > Q\} \dashrightarrow 1,$$

then the system must be secure in the sense outlined above. That is, the best that h can do is allow the enemy to make a list of Q possible meanings of C and to choose M′ randomly from this list; clearly for large Q the probability that M′ = M is small.

Another related measure of security arises when, for $E(K_1,M_1) = C_1$ as above, there is a key $K_2 \neq K_1$ such that $E(K_2,M_1) = C_1$. Thus, even though h may reveal the pair (M_1,C_1) it does not reveal the key used to encipher M_1.

Formally, if $P_C(K)$ and $P_C(M)$ represent the conditional probabilities of key K and message M given ciphertext C has been received, then the message equivocation $H_C(M)$ and key equivocation $H_C(K)$ are defined by:

$$H_C(X) = -\sum P(E,X)\log P_E(X),$$

where the summation is over E,K if X=K and E,M if X=M.

From the discussion above, an unconditionally secure system must have <u>incoherent</u> key streams. That is, the entropy of each key symbol must be at least as great as the average information content per symbol of the message. This condition is met by the Vernam cipher with a random nonrepeating key tape. Consider messages of length N in a language with rate R and let the rate of the key alphabet be R_K; then unconditional security requires

$$RN \leq R_K\sigma(N),$$

where $\sigma(N)$ is the minimal length key needed to encipher messages of size N. This condition is clearly satisfied by Vernam ciphers.

Finally, it is evident that the minimal amount of plaintext required for unique solution of a cipher can be made large by decreasing the redundancy of the language. At D=0, the cryptosystem admits no intersymbol dependencies (e.g., the output of a perfect source coder); unfortunately for such a system all errors go undetected, so the authorization and integrity problems are unsolvable for the cipher.

2.4 Feasibility of Cryptanalysis. So much for omnipotent enemies -- although we can get perfectly usable ciphers, the only provably secure system have severe drawbacks. What does it mean to limit the power of the enemy to feasible computation? To be precise, we must introduce the basic language of computational complexity theory. It seems fair to restrict the computational abilities of the enemy to effective procedures, that is, procedures that can be executed on computers. In solving a problem S on an idealized machine, the enemy will either fail to solve S or will solve it by using a finite amount of computational resources, such as time or memory. We will limit our attention to time as the resource, and denote by T(I) the amount of time taken on the idealized machine to solve instance I of S (forgetting for the moment about the units of time and the particular technology assumed in the idealized machine). We also assume that it is possible to consistently assign a measure of size to instances of problems. For example size(I) might be the number of bits required to represent I using a standard encoding of numbers, punctuation, etc. In this case, we usually simply write |I| for size(I). The number of instances of a given problem of some fixed size n is finite, so there is a number T(n) which is a lub on the set

$$\{T(I) \mid size(I) = n\}.$$

The _worst case complexity_ of the indicated solution to the problem is completely described by the function T(n). Notice that the units of measured time can only determine T(n) up to a constant; that is, a rescaling of time units is a constant multiple of the given units. By the same token, a change in computing technology can be expected to change the running time of a given algorithm by only a constant factor (e.g., the popular representation of the advance of technology is the factor increase in computing speed). In summary, it seems enough to know about the growth rate of T(n) up to a constant factor. Therefore, we will characterize T(n) by its order: $T(n) = O(g(n))$ if there is a constant c such that $T(n) \leq c \cdot g(n)$ for all $n > n_0$. On the other hand, if every solution to S has worst case complexity $T(n) \geq g(n)$ for infinitely many values of n, then the complexity of S cannot be O(g(n)), so g(n) is a _lower bound_ on the complexity of S.

Assessing feasibility in computation is based on empirical observations of time bounds of algorithms. A problem is said to be _feasibly solvable_ if the running time of a solution is upper bounded by a _polynomial_ function of problem size. Examples of feasible problems are sorting lists of n ordered objects (complexity $O(n(\log_2 n))$) and determining planarity of graphs (complexity O(n)). This does not imply that all polynomial running times are practically feasible, since n^{1000} is an exceedingly long running time for even modestly large n. But we do mean that polynomial growth in problems that we encounter _on a daily basis_ is sufficient for computational tractability. On the other hand, nonpolynomial running times are very restrictive. Algorithms with nonpolynomial running times prohibit (in general) all but the smallest instances, so it is usual to call problems with nonpolynomial lower bound on their running times _intractable_.

Among the intractable problems which are frequently encountered in mathematics, operations research and computer science are those that are solved by backtrack search procedures. Among these problems are the ones for which the backtrack search tree can always be bounded in depth by a polynomial function of the size of the input problem. The class of (suitably encoded) problems which are solvable in polynomial time is denoted by the letter **P** while problems that can be solved by polynomial depth backtrack search are denoted by **NP**. Clearly every problem in **P** is also in **NP**. At the present time it is not known if there are polynomially bounded algorithms for all problems in **NP**, but since **NP** contains some very difficult problems, it seems likely that many problems in **NP** have nonpolynomial lower bounds and are truly intractable. In **NP** are problems which are, in a formal sense, the most difficult problems in **NP**, the _NP-complete problems_. An NP-complete problem is remarkable in the following respect: if an NP-complete problem admits no polynomial solution, then obviously **P** ≠ **NP**, but if it is solvable in polynomial time then that polynomial time algorithm automatically yields a polynomial time algorithm for all problems in **NP** and so **P** = **NP**. At present, it is not known whether or not **P** = **NP**; however, it is widely believed that **P** ≠ **NP**. In that case, no NP-complete problem is in **P** and hence, no such problem has an efficient solution.

An example of an NP-complete problem is the _knapsack problem_. An instance of the knapsack problem is given by an integer S (the 'knapsack') and n integers $w_1, \ldots, w_n$ (the 'objects') The problem is to determine whether or not the knapsack can be filled by some subset of the given objects. In more convenient terms: given S and n-vector w, does there exist a binary vector x such that w $\cdot$ x = S? The best known algorithms for the 0/1 knapsack problem have running times of order $2^{(n/2)}$ or worse, although there are efficient solutions for special cases of w.

There are also difficult problems in NP that are not NP complete. For example, factorization of large integers into prime factors is at the current time thought to be intractable: the best known bounds are on the order of

$$e^{\sqrt{\ln(n)\ln(\ln(n))}},$$

where n is the number being factored. Another important, apparently complex, problem is taking logarithms in finite fields. In a Galois Field GF(p) for a prime p, exponentiation can be carried out by 2log(p) multiplications, but computing logarithms requires an exponential number of multiplications.

This last example points to another property of NP problems that make them important to cryptographers -- as opposed to, say, a problem which has *provably* exponential complexity: it is easy to verify that a solution has been found. To verify that one has obtained a logarithm in GF(p), it is necessary only to exponentiate the reputed logarithm, and we have already remarked that this operation has an efficient algorithm. Although it may be hard to find the factors of a composite number, the factors can be verified to yield the composite by a single multiplication of n bit numbers which can be carried out in time proportional to n(logn)(loglog n). Finally, a proposed solution vector x to a knapsack problem can be verified by carrying out the dot product in time proportional to n.

Most of the current activity in cryptographic theory is based on the following principle: the cryptanalytic function h should be computationally intractable (a hard **NP** problem, an **NP**-complete problem, etc.). We will examine this principle more critically in Section 2.6.

Secure cryptosystems based on the 'feasibility' model of cryptanalysis must satisfy certain minimal requirements. Let $E_K(.) = E(K,.)$ and $D_{K'}(.) = D(K',.)$, where K' is the key required for decryption. Then the cryptosystem must satisfy 1-4 (5 is a technical requirement which will play a role in certain protocols).

1. For each message M, $D_{K'}(E_K(M)) = M$,
2. E_K is computationally tractable,
3. $D_{K'}$ is computationally tractable,
4. D is concealed from an enemy who knows E (i.e., K but not K') by a computationally intractable problem,
5. for each message M, $E_K(D_{K'}(M)) = M$.

For such cryptosystems the information theoretic model of security does apply -- the enemy may indeed be able to break the cipher if the feasibility of the process of computing h is factored out of the model. But if h is intractable, growing in complexity say at an exponential rate, then by providing h with problems of large enough size, the resource bounds on any algorithm for h can be made impossibly large, thus separating the enemy from the messages (or, equivalently from the knowlege of the deciphering key K'). This is guaranteed by condition 4. Condition 1 simply insures that D and E behave correctly as ciphers, while condition 5, which says that E and D commute is a technical property not required to insure secrecy. This condition is required, however, to give the system security from certain threats to authorization or integrity. Conditions 2 and 3 represent the commonsense requirement that E and D both be efficiently computable, so that the encryption/decryption devices can run at rates which are limited by the transmission capacity of the communications medium and not by requirement of the cryptosystem design.

2.5 Modern Block Ciphers. From the point of view of the cryptanalyst, block ciphers increase the rate of the language being enciphered. This removes, for example, any reasonable possibility of ciphertext only attack by statistical means, since the basic unit of transmission has no direct relationship to the underlying language. On the other hand, dealing with blocks of tens of bits -- sometimes hundreds of bits -- in a single operation is beyond all but the most sophisticated mechanical transmitting devices and certainly beyond human capabilities. It is only through electronically implemented cryptosystems that block ciphers become feasible.

A simple device which at first sight might seem to give a very good block cipher is a maximal length linear feedback shift register (LFSR) as shown in Figure 2.5.

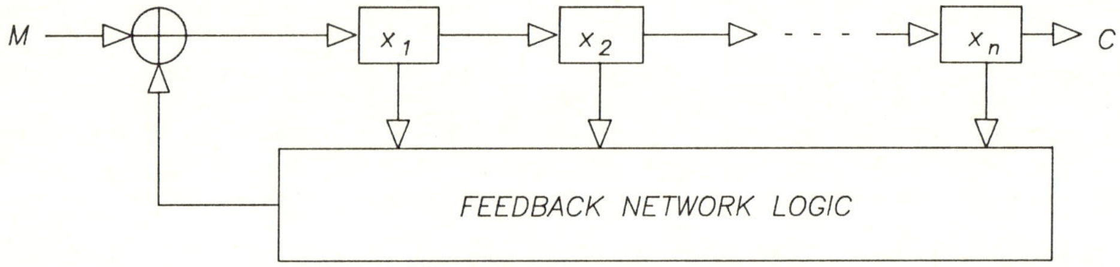

Figure 2.5
Logical Organization of LFSR

The LFSR implements a polynomial f(x) with coefficients from the field of integers modulo a prime p. Furthermore, $f(x) \mid (x^n-1)$, where $n=p^t-1$, if f is of degree t.

Since LFSR's produce output which meets several of the statistical tests for randomness, they are often suggested as block ciphers. To use a LFSR as an enciphering device, an n bit message is loaded into the shift register $x_1,\ldots x_n$. The device is then stepped through some number of steps greater than n and the output C is read from the register. Decipherment is carried out by stepping the inverse logic through the same number of steps. Although the output is apparently random, the fact that LFSR's implement polynomials makes them quite susceptible to known plaintext attacks. An enemy who knows some plaintext-cipher text pairs can set up a system of 2n linear equations and solve the system to obtain the feedback logic and the polynomial coefficients which allow him to duplicate both the encryption and decryption devices.

Since LFSR's reveal their keys too easily, block ciphers must be sought which satisfy the basic computional requirements outlined above. Surprisingly, the place to begin looking for such an algorithm is the simple monographic substitution cipher which was discarded as insecure for stream ciphers. Random substitution alphabets for blocks of n bits can be realized by a device such as the one shown in Figure 2.6.

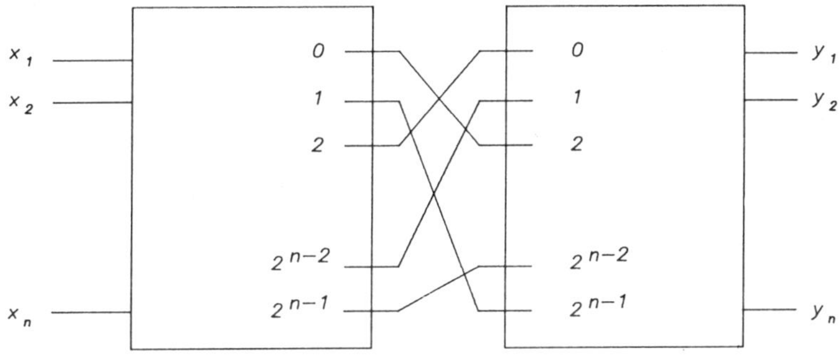

Figure 2.6
Substitution Box

The substitution algorithm consists of two devices: one to transform an n-bit block into a corresponding base n value by signaling on one of the 2^n output lines, and the other to carry out the reverse transformation. The base n output lines of the first device can be connected to the base n input lines of the second device in any of n! ways. There is a simple frequency analysis of such a scheme for values of n between 4 and 5 (the number of bits required to represent the standard alphabet) and the information theoretic cryptanalysis of such a scheme paints a very dismal picture. But size is an important component here. For large values of n (say, n = 128) the frequency attack is no longer possible. However, such a device is impossible to build since it requires 2^{128} internal switches. By cascading a number of more economical devices, it is possible to create a product polygraphic block substitution cipher that has many of the advantages of the n = 128 device.

Such a scheme is shown in Figure 2.7.

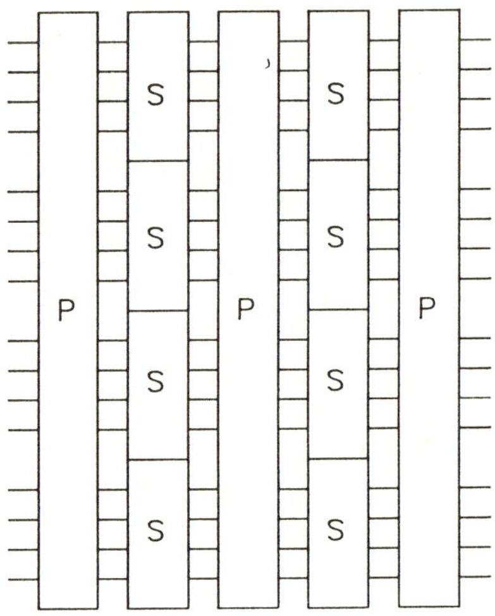

Figure 2.7.
A Product Cipher S/P Network

This is essentially the design of the IBM Lucifer system. The choice of n for each substitution box is quite small (n=4), although the block size for the entire device is large. A key for such a system is a specification for each permutation box, of which the 64! or 128! permutations is to be selected and for each substitution box which of the 16 substitutions is to be performed. It is possible to construct a S/P network that behaves quite badly by choosing keys which permute the plaintext bits in the cipher text. This permutation can be discovered by chosen plaintext analysis of blocks that contain a single 1. Tracing the path of the bit through the network is then simply a process of observing the output wires for the single on bit. Lucifer permanently keys each P and each S box with "good" keys; for example, each S box is specified by selecting a substitution from two permanently keyed substitutions -- call them S_0 and S_1. So to describe a key, one sets a binary string $b_1 b_2 \ldots b_k$, where $b_i = 0$ if the ith S box is S_0 and $b_i = 1$ otherwise.

The Lucifer system is a high-quality block cipher. It is, however, not now considered to be a secure system -- Lucifer's operating environment assumes that keys (which are contained on passcards issued to bank customers) cannot be read and altered by enemies. Lucifer also implements a strong form of information theoretically secure (for authorization) encipherment, but cannot be widely used for other cryptographic tasks (cf. Chapter 4).

2.5.1 The Data Encryption Standard. In 1977 the U.S. National Bureau of Standards (NBS) issued a Data Encryption Standard (DES). The DES algorithm is a block cipher developed by IBM based on an S/P network as in the Lucifer system described above. The intention in issuing DES was to provide a cryptographic standard to be used for secure data transmission for all but national security-related data. Figure 2.8 is a schematic diagram of the DES algorithm as it was issued by NBS.

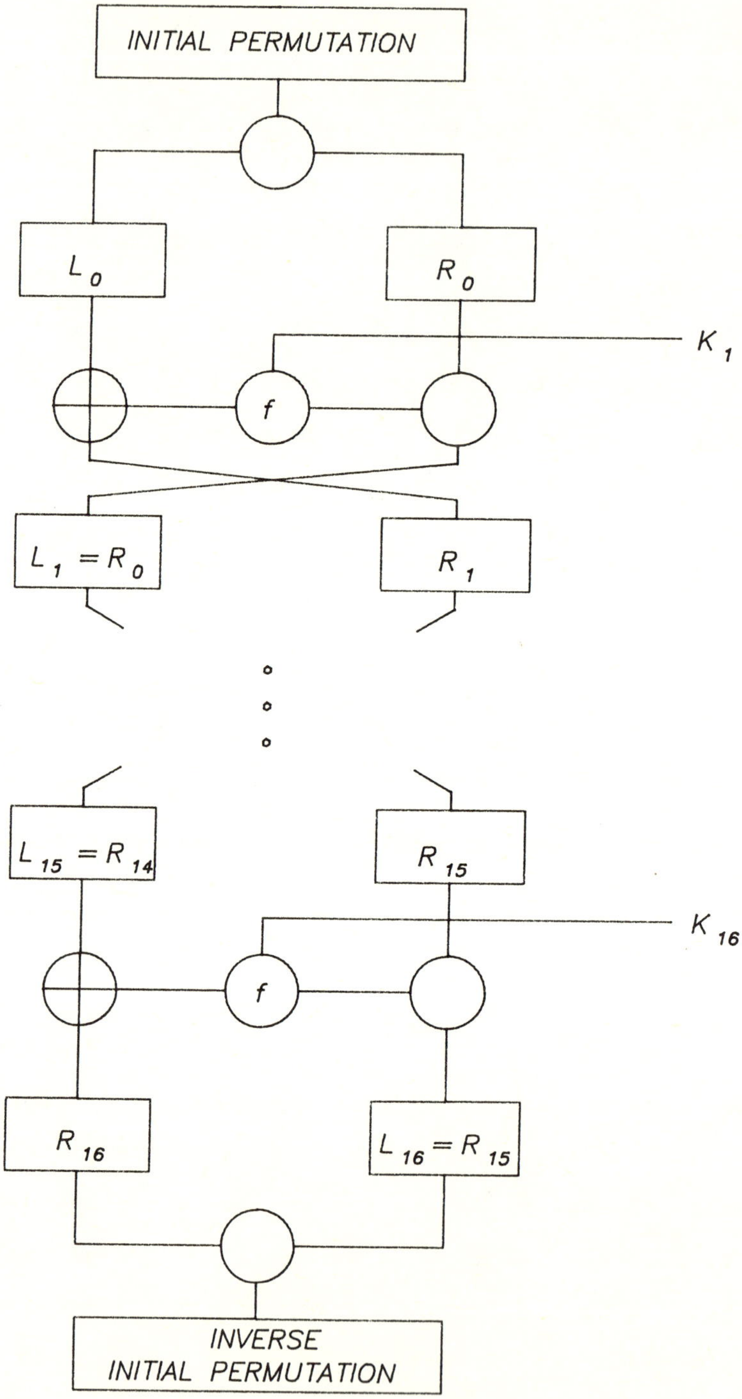

Figure 2.8
The DES Algorithm

Briefly, DES enciphers 64 bit blocks of plaintext using a 64 bit key (56 bits of key and 8 parity bits). Encryption is by 16 separate rounds of encipherment, each round a product cipher under the control of a 48 bit key. That is, each round uses a distinct 48 bit key $K_1, \ldots K_{16}$ obtained by a scheduling algorithm from the external key K. To decipher, the keys are scheduled in reverse order using the same external key K. The cryptographic function E(K,M) = C can be defined in terms of an equation

$$IP^{-1}(F)IP(M) = C,$$

where IP is the initial input permutation. F represents the portion of the cipher that depends on the key K and is described by the function f and a key scheduling algorithm KS. f is a product cipher (a S/P network). It is sufficient to describe only the first round since the remaining rounds behave identically. The 64 bits of the initial permutation are split into two 32 bit blocks, bits 1 through 32 being designated the L_0 block and bits 33 through 64 the R_0 block, so at the start of this round IP(M) = L_0R_0. KS produces the first 48 bit key K_1. The output of the round is a block L_1R_1 which is also the input to the next round. These 32 bit blocks are described by the equations:

$$L_1 = R_0$$

$$R_1 = L_0 \oplus f(R_0, K).$$

After the 16th round, the blocks are permuted to obtain C. The key scheduling algorithm is a complex sequential shifting process; since it has little cryptographic significance, we will not describe it. The same algorithm can be used for deciphering as long as the output permutation is an inverse of the input permutation, the same key is used and if L',R' are the output of a round:

$$R = L'$$

$$L = R' \oplus f(L', K_i).$$

The symmetry in the encryption/decryption process can be seen by writing the rounds in reverse order. Let $K_1, \ldots, K_{16}$ be the 48 bit keys produced by the key scheduling algorithm. Then

$$L_n = R_{n-1}$$

$$R_n = L_{n-1} \oplus f(R_{n-1}, K_n),$$

and

$$R_{n-1} = L_n$$

$$L_{n-1} = R_n \oplus f(L_n, K_n).$$

Clearly, the scheduled keys are used in reverse order and in the forward direction the permuted input block is L_0R_0, while the preoutput before final permutation is $R_{16}L_{16}$. During decipherment $R_{16}L_{16}$ is the permuted input and L_0R_0 is the preoutput.

The product cipher f is described in Figure 2.9. The function accepts a 32 bit input block and outputs 8 blocks of 6 bits each, where each 6 bit block has its bits selected from the input block according to a fixed selection table. After combination with the scheduled key, the blocks are passed to 8 substitution boxes which compress the blocks, substitute and produce 4 bit output blocks. This 32 bit output is then subjected to a permutation and the result is returned as the result of the f operation.

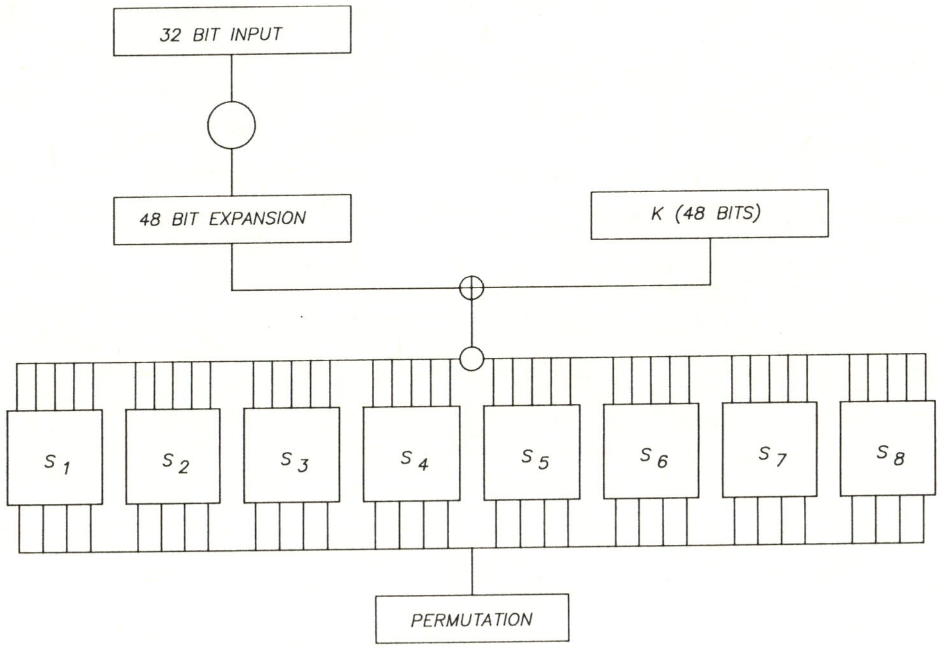

Figure 2.9
The Calculation of f

Many standard tests of cryptographic strength have been applied to the DES algorithm with positive results. DES exhibits, for example, strong intersymbol dependence: a small change in the input message causes massive changes in the output cipher.

DES can be used as a stream cipher simply by observing that it is a good generator of random numbers. The key K is used as a seed, and subsequent outputs are recycled through the system to produce a long pseudo random key which can be used as a Vernam cipher key. This process is sometimes called <u>feedback chain encipherment</u>.

2.5.2 Cryptanalysis. In the information-theoretic model, DES does not exhibit strong security. By computing equivocation for DES under various attacks, it can be shown that one or two blocks determine a key even if only ciphertext is available to the enemy. The key size of the standard has been criticized. The crux of the problem with DES is that the 56 bit key size seems to admit a known plaintext analysis by an enemy with massive -- but feasible -- computational resources. The analysis is simply a brute force search. Suppose that known message M is enciphered using DES with key K and that E(K,M) = C. To discover K, the cryptanalyst deciphers C with each of the 2^{56} possible keys. When he discovers M, he stops and announces the key. Since 2^{56} is approximately 10^{17}, this exhaustive search sounds prohibitive. But it has been argued that special purpose hardware can be constructed to enable a million parallel searches to take place in about twelve hours. With available technology such a machine can be constructed for about $20 million. With some reasonable assumptions about the operating environment this cost can be amortized to about $5,000 per solution -- well within the range of a determined enemy! NBS has argued vigorously against the feasibility of this analysis.

No one has yet questioned the practical security of DES-style algorithms. It seems, for example, that simply by increasing the key size from 56 to 128 an exhaustive cryptanalysis is ruled out.

2.5.3 Public Key Systems. The cryptosystems given above all have the property that the encryption key K and the decryption key K′ are the same. They are conventional ciphers. At first blush, it is hard to imagine how requiring $K \neq K'$ can help the cryptosystem since differing encryption and decryption keys would require an extra exchange of keys and therefore an extra possibility of compromise. Consider the key exchanges in an n-person conventional cryptosystem. To provide for pairwise secure communications $O(n^2)$ keys must be exchanged. Our goal is to exploit the fact that $K \neq K'$ to reduce the "exhanges" to $O(n)$ keys.

In any case, the entire question may be irrelevant since it is not at all clear that there exists any ciphers that satisfy conditions 1 - 5: the troublesome condition seems to be the condition that the deciphering algorithm be hard to infer from the enciphering algorithm. More exactly, if K' is fixed and a function f(K') is used to derive an enciphering key K, then knowing E_K should not reveal $f^{-1}(K)$. Such a function is <u>one-way</u> in that it is easy to compute but hard to invert.

Given such functions, it is easy to see how a scheme based on 1 - 5 might operate. All participants in the cryptosystem agree to derive (according to special rules that depend on the cipher) a pair of keys satisfying 1 - 5 -- call them K and K'. The enciphering key K is made public; for example, K can be published in a directory which is distributed to all users. The deciphering key K' is kept secret, however. Suppose that A wants to communicate with B. A consults the public directory to find B's encipherment key K, P_B. A then computes E(K,M) = C and sends C to B. When B receives C, he uses his secret key $K' = S_B$ to recover M = D(K',C). Since K' is concealed by a computationally intractable problem from anyone who does not know K', the message is secure from all attacks. Such a cryptosystem is called a <u>public key</u> cryptosystem.

2.5.4 The RSA Algorithm. At this time it is not known whether or not <u>provably</u> secure public key encryption algorithms exist (cf. Section 2.6). There have been several proposals for algorithms whose security has the essentially the same status as the **P=NP** problem. The first such algorithm to be announced was the RSA algorithm.

The RSA algorithm depends on some simple number theory. We use the familiar notation $\phi(n)$ to denote the Euler function. Clearly, if p is a prime number, then $\phi(p) = p-1$. Also, if p and q are primes, then $\phi(pq) = (p-1)(q-1)$.

The <u>private</u> key is a triple (p,q,d), where p and q are large primes and the <u>public</u> key is a pair (n,e), where $n=p \cdot q$. Notice that the public key does not mention the factorization of n. Since p and q are prime $\phi(n) = (p-1)(q-1)$ can be computed quickly. The remaining portions of the keys are derived as follows. Let e be chosen so that $(e,\phi(n)) = 1$; e.g., e may be any prime between max(p,q) and n-1. To obtain d, the Euclidean Algorithm can be used to find integers d, b such that

$$de + b\phi(n) = 1.$$

Thus, a d for which

$$de = 1 \bmod \phi(n)$$

is determined.

Encipherment is carried out on a message M by

$$M^e \bmod n = c$$

and decipherment is carried out by

$$C^d \bmod n = M'.$$

We first show that encipherment and decipherment behave properly; i.e. $M = M'$.

Two preliminary facts are necessary. The first is Fermat's Little Theorem: if p is prime and x is an integer which does not contain p as a factor,

then

$$x^{p-1} \equiv 1 \bmod p.$$

The second fact is a technical lemma. Suppose $n = pq$ and that p and q are both relatively prime to x. Then

$$x^{\phi(n)} \equiv 1 \bmod p\,q.$$

To see why, consider the following instances of Fermat's Little Theorem:

$$x^{p-1} \equiv 1 \bmod p \text{ and } x^{q-1} \equiv 1 \bmod q.$$

Since

$$x^{\phi(n)} = x^{(p-1)(q-1)} = (x^{p-1})^{q-1} = (x^{q-1})^{p-1},$$

we have

$$x^{\phi(n)} = 1 \bmod p \text{ and } x^{\phi(n)} = 1 \bmod q.$$

Since $p \mid x^{\phi(n)}-1$ and $q \mid x^{\phi(n)} - 1$,

$$x^{\phi(n)}-1 \equiv 0 \bmod pq,$$

giving the result.

We now claim that

$$M^{ed} \equiv M \bmod n.$$

There are two cases according to whether or not M and n are relatively prime. If $(M,n) = 1$, then

$$M^{ed} = M^{1+c\cdot\phi(n)} \equiv M \bmod n.$$

Therefore, suppose that $M = py$, where $(y,q) = 1$. Then

$$M^{ed} - M = M^{1+c\cdot\phi(n)} - M = M(M^{c\cdot\phi(n)} - 1).$$

By the technical lemma,

$$M^{ed} - M \equiv 0 \bmod p\, q.$$

How is condition 4 satisfied? If n can be factored then d can be determined from e as described above. It does not follow that determining d from e requires the factorization of n, although there does not appear to be any way around it.

Choosing large enough primes to satisfy the security requirements is fairly simple. There are already hardware devices available which will generate prime numbers of a hundred bits or more in several seconds.

There is very little cryptanalytical experience with the RSA algorithm. Of course, it is not known whether or not factorization is an intractable problem, but there are certainly no fast algorithms in existence today, and it seems safe to assume that this situation will not change soon.

The RSA algorithm may have unfortunate behavior in some

cases. It is known, for example, that for every public key (n,e) at least nine messages will be encrypted as themselves. In addition, there are very bad choices of e which leave half of the messages unaffected by encryption. This can be avoided by choosing <u>safe</u> primes p and q: for example p = 2p'+1 is a safe prime. In addition, there may be iterative attacks. A cryptanalyst may successively encrypt M^e until he obtains plaintext. To avoid this attack, p must be chosen so that p-1 has a large prime factor p' and p'-1 has a large prime factor p".

2.5.5 Related Algorithms. Another public key system can be based on the computation of logarithms in finite fields. A user selects a secret integer less than the number p-1 for the prime p (call it X) and a public key

$$Y = a^X \pmod p,$$

where $a \in GF(p)$. To transmit from user A with public key X to user B with public key x, A computes

$$a^{Xx} \pmod p = y^X \pmod p$$

$$= Y^x \pmod p,$$

where Y and y are the secret keys of A and B respectively. To compromise this system, the enemy is required to compute logarithms base a in GF(p):

$$Y^{\log_a y} \pmod p.$$

A more subtle example is based on the knapsack problem. This algorithm is based on the following special case of the knapsack problem (find boolean vector x such that $S = a \cdot x$). If, for all values of i,

$$a_i > a_1 + a_2 + \ldots + a_{i-1},$$

then $x_i = 1$ iff either of the following two conditions are met:

1. $i = n$ and $S > a_n$, or

2. $i < n$ and

$$S - \sum_{j=1}^{i-1} x_j a_j \geq a_i$$

The public key in this case is a vector a. To send x to a user with public key a, a user sends $S = x \cdot a$. Thus recovering x is equivalent to solving a knapsack problem. The owner of a, however, has chosen a to correspond to another vector a' which he keeps secret and which satisfies (1) and (2) above so that $S' = a' \cdot x$ can be easily solved. He chooses values of m and w so that the multiplicative inverse of w (mod m) exists and derives a from a' by the rule:

$$a_i = wa_i' \pmod m.$$

Therefore, to decrypt S, the designer need only compute

$$S' = vS \bmod m,$$

where v is the inverse of w. This, in turn, is equal to

$$x_1a_1' + x_2a_2' + \ldots \pmod m,$$

and if m is larger than the sum of the components of a', then

$$S' = x \cdot a'$$

which is an easy case of the knapsack problem.

Shamir has recently provided a successful cryptanalysis of the knapsack-based public key cryptosystem. Specifically, Shamir has shown that whenever the public key $(a_1,\ldots,a_n)$ has the property that each a_i is a modular multiple of a sequence $(b_1,\ldots,b_n)$ such that

$$b_i > b_1+b_2+\ldots+b_{i-1},$$

Then almost all equations

$$\sum_{i=1}^{n} x_i a_i = c$$

can be found in polynomial time, giving an efficient method of recovering plaintext $(x_1,\ldots,x_n)$ from ciphertext c. A fast integer programming algorithm is used to find a real number $d \varepsilon (0,1)$ such that a necessary condition on the values m and w used in the knapsack algorithm is that $m/w \ \varepsilon \ [\alpha,\alpha+\varepsilon]$ for small ε. Next n^2 subintervals (β_i,γ_i) of $[\alpha,\alpha,+\varepsilon]$ are constructed so that if $m/w \ \varepsilon \ (\beta_i,\gamma_i)$, then m, w can be used in the knapsack algorithm. Since at least one pair of integers m, w is known to exist, at least one (β_i,γ_i) must be nonempty. An efficient diophantine approximation algorithm locates the smallest m and w such that m/w is in some (β_i,γ_i). Notice that Shamir's algorithm does not necessarily construct the <u>same</u> m, w used in the original knapsack. This argument has recently be extended to cover various generalizations of the knapsack cipher, which must now be regarded as insecure.

There have been efforts to refine the RSA algorithm. The

basic rationale of the RSA approach is to force the cryptanalyst to solve an equation of the form

$$x^m = y \pmod{n}.$$

If it is hard to solve such a congruence, then it should be harder still to solve a system of the form

$$f_i(x) = y_i \pmod{n},$$

where the function f_i are 'difficult' functions in the ring of algebraic numbers $\mathbf{Q}(\sqrt{s})$ for s a square-free rational integer. Let n=pq for large primes p,q and

$$(s/p) = (s/q) = -1,$$

where (α/β) denotes the Legendre symbol, so that s is a quadratic non-residue mod p and q, and $\phi(n) = (p^2-1)(q^2-1)$ so that $m_1m_2=1 (\mathrm{mod}\ \phi(n))$ is as hard as factorization. Identify the point (a,b) for rational a,b with $a+b\sqrt{s}$. A public key is a triple (s,n,e). The corresponding private key is (p,q,d), where,

$$ed \equiv 1 \bmod (p^2-1)(q^2-1).$$

Letting * represent pointwise defined multiplication in $\mathbf{Q}(\sqrt{s})$ (i.e., (x,y)*(u,v) = (a,b) when a = xu+syv(mod n) and b = xv+yu(mod n)) encryption of a message M is defined by

$$M^e \bmod n$$

and decryption of ciphertext c is defined by

$$c^d \bmod n,$$

where exponentiation is the iteration of *.

Factorization in Z (as in RSA) or in $Q(\sqrt{s})$ is sufficient to allow successful cryptanalysis of the public key systems, but it may not be necessary. At present, no functions that are suitable for communication are known which are provably equivalent to factorization.

There is, however, a public key function that is suitable for certain protocols that has the property that cryptanalyzing it implies factoring. The public key K is a pair (n,b), where n is the product of two large primes p and q and $0 \leq b < n$.

The encryption of a message $M \leq n/2^k$, for some fixed k is

$$C = E_{(n,b)}(M) = M(M+b) \bmod n.$$

The receiver of the cipher text C knows p, q and also that

$$C = x(x+b) \bmod n.$$

Hence, Berlekamp's Algorithm can be used to solve

$$x(x+b) = C \bmod p$$

and

$$x(x+b) = C \bmod q,$$

and, by Chinese remaindering, obtain x_1, x_2, x_3, x_4 so that

$$x_i^2 + bx_i = E_{(n,b)} \bmod n.$$

There are two possibilities. If only one of the solutions x_i (in binary) ends in k zeroes, then $x=x_i/2^k$ is the proper decryption of C. If, on the other hand, more than one of the solutions ends in k zeroes, then C decrypts ambiguously. This 4-1 nature of decryption may make this function unsuitable for normal communications. However if k is large enough, the second case rarely arises.

The cryptanalytic function is h(y), where:

$$y = E_{(n,b)}(x),\ x \leq n/2^k \text{ implies } h(y) = x.$$

Notice that the behavior of h is unspecified when y is not in the proper form. Computing such an h is equivalent to factorization by the following argument. Suppose that the system can be cryptanalyzed. Pick a random x and let $y = x^2 \bmod n$. Suppose that the cryptanalyst has obtained in a z such that $y = z^2 \bmod n$, so that $x^2 = z^2 \bmod n$. Then a factorization of n is obtained as follows. If $x \neq \pm z \bmod n$, then by computing (x-z,n) or (x+z,n), we get a factor of n. If, on the other hand, $x = \pm z$ modulo n, then since x was chosen randomly, we have equality with probability at most 1/2. If we repeatedly select random values of x, we will quickly get $x \neq \pm z$ and thus factor n.

Public key cryptosystems are also susceptible to various styles of attack that do not address the strength of the complex problem used to define the public and private keys. These are attacks on the _protocols_ used to implement the cryptosystem and are discussed in Chapter 4.

2.6 Intractability and Cryptanalysis. Such problems as factoring integers, the travelling salesman problem, graph coloring, and integer programming are all in the class NP. One way of looking at a backtrack procedure for solving these problems is to look at the branching backtrack tree describing the backtrack search. At each step of the backtrack procedure, the search algorithm must 'guess' which elementary item is to be considered next in the search. The algorithm proceeds with the search with this item under consideration until one of two things happens. Either the search is successful (in which case it terminates) or the search is unsuccessful. In the latter case, the procedure 'backtracks'; that is, it proceeds to the most recent point at which it is possible to undo the effects of a wrong guess and makes a new guess. If it is not possible to make a new guess, then the algorithm terminates unsuccessfully.

Thus, a backtrack search algorithm, B, running on an input I, of size n, defines a set of possible computations C(B,I). If the search is supposed to determine whether or not $I \in S$, then each computation in C(B,I) should terminate and announce either $I \in S$ or $I \notin S$. The algorithm is said to <u>accept</u> I in time T(n) if there is a sequence of guesses in C(B,I) which leads to the result "$I \in S$" in at most T(n) elementary operations. B accepts S in time T if for every $I \in S$, B accepts I in time T(n). Formally, the set **NP** is the set of problems S which are accepted by algorithms in time $T(n) = O(n^k)$ for $k \geq 0$.

The theoretical superstructure of computational intractability is essentially the conjecture that **P** does not equal **NP**. There are, in addition, intermediate notions that often prove to be useful in the theory. One such notion is that of a **co-NP** problem. Suppose that S is simply a subset of a fixed reference set U (for example, if S is the set of composites, then U may be the set of all integers in some suitable notation). If $S \in$ **NP**, then it may be useful to consider the set $U-S = \overline{S}$. $\overline{S}$ is said to be in the class **co-NP**. There is a characterization of these classes that may be helpful in visualizing the relationship between them. One may think of S as defined by a predicate:

$$I \varepsilon S \text{ iff } (\exists y)(|y| \leq n^k \wedge B(I,y)),$$

where y is intended to denote the sequence of backtrack guesses and B(I,y) is **true** exactly when the polynomial time algorithm B on input I will evaluate "I ε S" when the guesses y are made. Then clearly,

$$I \varepsilon \overline{S} \text{ iff } (\forall y)(|y| \leq n^k \Rightarrow \neg B(n,y)).$$

How essential is this change in logical quantification? If S is in **P**, then clearly $\overline{S}$ is in **P**, since the backtrack procedure need not guess at all. On the other hand, there are problems in **NP** and co-**NP** which appear to be difficult indeed (although not necessarily **NP**-complete). Factorization is one such problem. Although there are **NP**-style algorithms to determine both the set of primes and the set of composites, the problem of factoring in polynomial time remains unsolved.

Thus, theoreticians like to add a corollary conjecture to the **P** = **NP** conjecture; that is, **NP** = co-**NP**. If **P** = **NP**, then **NP** = co-**NP**.

Let us now return to our axioms for D and E given in Section 2.4. We would like to know exactly how complex the problem is which separates D and E in a public key system. If the problem of determining D from E is, for example, **NP**-complete, then we have proved (modulo the **P** vs. **NP** conjecture) that the the cryptanalysis must solve an intractable problem.

But deriving D from E cannot be equivalent to an NP-complete problem because of the following theorem: the computational task to deriving D from E is in **NP** and **co-NP**. Thus if the cryptanalytical problem is NP-complete, it follows that NP=co-NP, which is considered to be just as unlikely as P=NP. To see why the theorem is true, let h be the cryptanalytic function. Since h^{-1} is simply the process of computing enciphering keys from deciphering keys, practice dicatates the following conditions.

1. $|h^{-1}(i)| = |i|$,
2. $h^{-1}: N \dashrightarrow N$ is a bijection
3. h^{-1} is in P.

Define the set

$$S = \{(n,m) | h(n) > m\}.$$

First, S must be in NP: a backtrack algorithm B can guess an $|n|$ bit integer i, verify that $h^{-1}(i)=n$ and accept only if $i>m$. Second S must be in co-NP since there is a similar algorithm B* that accepts only if $i \geq m$. Now h(n) has $2^{|n|}$ possible values. But in order to avoid exhaustively searching all values, we need only use B and B* to perform a binary search. That is, search for x in an interval of s numbers, by simply successively bisecting into subintervals at the midpoints t_0, t_1, ..., $t_{\log s}$, where the ith subinterval S_i is determined by the following rule: if $x < t_{i-1}$, then

$$S_i = \{j \in S_{i-1} \mid j < t_{i-1}\},$$

otherwise,

$$S_i = \{j \in S_{i-1} \mid j > t_{i-1}\}.$$

This uses at most $|n|$ operations. Thus h is in both **NP** and co-**NP**.

While it is desirable to have E and D be separated by a complex problem, there are as yet no examples of such a function. Failing this, we have been reduced to a kind of argument by analogy. We have argued that breaking a particular system is "similar" to solving other hard problems (including some that are **NP**-complete). Such arguments while useful in practice fall far short of _proving_ the intractability of the cryptanalytic problem. As in the case of the classical ciphering problems, it is tempting to try to read too much into the _apparent_ difficulty of decipherment.

In the modern case, the safety of the cipher depends on a conjecture: perhaps it is false!

Moreover, even if **P** $\neq$ **NP**, none of the following are ruled out:

1. There is an algorithm for each **NP** problem that runs in $n^{t(n)}$ steps, where $t(n) \to \infty$ very slowly; Such an algorithm is not polynomially bounded, but might well be able to derive D from E;
2. there is a random algorithm that works in random polynomial time;
3. there is an algorithm that solves all instances of the travelling salesman problem of length $n \leq 10^{10}$ in n^3 steps; since 10^{10} is a generous bound on key size, such an algorithm could feasibly compute h;

4. there is an algorithm for each **NP** problem that solves 1% of the problem instances in polynomial time. For most applications this compromises the security of the deciphering key.

Thus, the question of whether or not **P = NP** seems to be a rather narrow one on which to rest cryptographic security, and it is probably best not to gain too much confidence from it alone since none of the above are ruled out by a proof that **P ≠ NP**.

We can see an example of this in the 4-1 encryption function which we showed to be as hard as factorization in Section 2.5. Let $E_1 = E_{(n_1,0)}$ and let $E_2 = E_{(n_2,0)}$, where n_1 and n_2 have distinct prime factors and $|n_1| = |n_2|$. Since frequent key change is commonly thought to be a good additional security measure, it is perhaps reasonable to ask whether or not putting $E_1(x)$ and $E_2(x)$ in the hands of the cryptanalyst will ever compromise the message. Notice carefully that the proof of equivalence to factorization says nothing at all about multiple systems, and so no contradiction arises. To see how the message can be compromised let

$$x^2 = a + yN$$

$$x^2 = b + zM$$

where $(N,M)=1$ and a,b are residues with $0 \leq M < N$. But, given a,b,N,M, x can be quickly determined. Notice

$$a - b = zM - yN.$$

Thus, by the Euclidean Algorithm, we can obtain

$$a - b = z_0M - y_0N,$$

for known z_0, y_0 with $|z_0| \leq N$ and $|y_0| \leq M$. Then

$$z = z_0 + tN$$

$$y = y_0 + tM$$

are the general solutions to the equations . It follows that

$$x^2 - a - y_0N = tNM,$$

so,

$$|x^2 - a - y_0N| \leq 3N^2.$$

Therefore t is at most 3N/M, but N and M are the same order of magnitude so only a constant number of t's need be tried to find x.

There is another threat to this function: a message may be <u>partially</u> decrypted without factoring the key. Let $E(x) = E_{(n,b)}(x)$. We will let the message be k bits in size -- say k=300 -- so that at 6 bits per character, 50 characters are encoded in a message. In the example of the cryptanalysis of Enigma we noted that the cryptanalysts were aided greatly by the stylized form of the plaintext. In modern electronic applications, the situation frequently occurs that series of highly similar messages are sent. For example EFT orders frequently differ only in the amount to be transferred, and many other messages are simply updated versions of previously sent messages. Thus, we may find applications for which cryptanalysis need only analyze messages that are close to each other in that they differ only in a fixed number of characters. We will consider the simplest case of this situation: x and y differ in at most one character. Notice that this case is equivalent to x = y+d, for some $d \in \Delta$, where $|\Delta| = 64 \cdot 50$. This is simply due to the fact that each character position can be changed by adding a suitable d and there are at most $64 \cdot 50$ such changes.

We now show that if x and y differ in at most one character, x and y can be recovered from E(x) and E(y) in polynomial time. Since $x = y+d$,

$$E(y) - E(x) = -x^2bx + [(x+d)^2+b(x+d)](\bmod n).$$

Thus,

$$E(y) - E(x) = 2dx + d^2 + bd \pmod n.$$

This is a linear equation and so can be solved for x. Notice that this result also does not lead to contradiction to the equivalence to factorization since if x and y are random messages they will only rarely differ in one character.

Chapter 4 describes additional attacks on cryptosystems which do not actually result in key compromise.

For conventional ciphers (those for which K=K'), computational intractability is no theoretical impediment at all. There are, for example, ciphers which are provably intractable in the sense that they are NP-complete, but which are easy to compromise. That is, there is a cipher with the following properties:

1. computing h under chosen plaintext attack is NP-complete,

2. given enough (M,C) pairs h can be efficiently com-

puted with probability approaching unity.

The cipher uses a key $k=(x_1,...x_n)$ of

$$m = \lceil \log_2(1+a_1+...+a_n]) \rceil,$$

and $A=(a_1,...,a_n)$ is known to the cryptanalyst.

To generate C from M:

1. generate a random vector R,
2. compute $S=A(K\oplus R)^T$
3. set $C=(M\oplus S_2,R)$, where S_2 is S encoded in binary.

Notice that the ciphertext is of length m+n. Knowledge of K insures easy decryption.

The cryptanalyst has available to him many pairs (M_i,C_i), where

$$C_i = (M_i\oplus S_i,R_i).$$

It is very likely that n of these will be such that

$$U_i = 1^n - 2R_i,$$

(where 1^n is a vector of n 1's) are linearly independent over the reals. This follows since the R_i' are randomly chosen. Now,

$$K\oplus R_i = K + R_i - 2K*R_i,$$

where * denotes component-wise multiplication. Thus,

$$K\oplus R_i = R_i^T K*U_i,$$

and, therefore,

$$S_i = A(K\oplus R_i)^T$$

$$= A(R_i + K*U_i)^T$$

$$= AR_i^T + A(K*U_i)^T$$

Now, letting $t_i = S_i - AR_i^T$, we obtain the following equations in matrix form:

$$\begin{bmatrix} t_1 \\ t_2 \\ \cdot \\ \cdot \\ \cdot \\ t_n \end{bmatrix} \begin{bmatrix} u_1 \\ u_2 \\ \cdot \\ \cdot \\ \cdot \\ u_n \end{bmatrix} \begin{bmatrix} a_1 & & & & \\ & a_2 & & & \\ & & \cdot & & \\ & & & \cdot & \\ & & & & a_n \end{bmatrix} = \begin{bmatrix} x_1 \\ x_2 \\ \cdot \\ \cdot \\ \cdot \\ x_n \end{bmatrix}$$

Since the U_i's are independent and all $a_i > 0$, it follows that we can easily solve for the key k.

2.7 Bibliographic Notes. The classic survey of conventional cryptography -- particularly its applications is [45]. For a more technical treatment of mathematical cryptography and cryptanalysis, a good treatment is [47], while an elementary survey of substitution ciphers is presented in [83]. The history of American involvement in diplomatic and military codes is available in [85], which has recently been reprinted. The account of how the Enigma code was broken is taken from [23].

The information theoretic approach to cryptography is due to Shannon [80]. Important recent contributions have also been made by Hellman [38]. The complexity theoretic approach to cryptanalysis was proposed in [27] and [56]; for a less technical survey, see also [39] and [40]. Computational complexity theory is presented in many modern computer science texts: [1] is representative. The concept of NP-complete problems originated with Karp in [46]. Public Key encryption was proposed by Diffie and Hellman in [27] and by Merkle in [56]. The RSA algorithm is due to Rivest, Shamir and Adelman [70]. Since then, there has been extensive literature on the mathematics of public key systems; see for example [51,58,74,78,79]. The algebraic number theory algorithm is due to Lipton [53], while the quadratic algorithm was proposed by Rabin as a signature scheme [67]. Critical analyses of public key systems have been presented in [41,65]. The results about weaknesses in certain public key algorithms are due to Blakely and Blakely [5]. For a survey article which relates conventional ciphers and public key systems, see [81].

The outlines of S/P network encryption is sketched in [32], where a description of the Lucifer system also appears. The DES algorithm can be obtained from the US Printing Office [61]. The cryptanalysis of DES was carried out by Hellman and is described in [28]. An extensive controversy has raged over this and other approaches to secure cryptosystems; accounts of these appear regularly in Science and other technical publications. The public-key encryption algorithms have also been popularized [34].

The relationship between NP and public key systems was developed in [7] and [31]. The example of an insecure system based on an NP-complete problem appears in [31]. Shamir's analysis of the knapsack algorithm was announced in [77].

3. Computer System Security Models

In this chapter, we will briefly survey security models which deal with computer system security. In contrast to the previous chapter, there is very little in the way of orderly development that can be seen in the field as a whole -- models and designs are motivated mainly by sets of competing requirements and costs, and concepts tend to reappear in several disguises. It is certain that the central issues have not yet been clearly articulated. Rather than try to give a complete picture of the state-of-the-art in computer system security, we will concentrate on models which have the most relevance for the protocol applications: the access control and multilevel security models for secure operating systems and the security models for statistical databases.

3.1 Operating System Models. Modern computer systems contain important information and unauthorized access can result in significant problems. One need only think of certain examples like electronic funds transfer systems, internal revenue service applications, and command and control computers used in military applications to realize the significance and scope of the problem of guaranteeing secure computation.

In the real world, there are many techniques used for penetrating systems which involve subverting people (or machines), tapping communication lines, and breaching physical security. In order to be able to approach the security problem in a mathematical way, we must make a number of simplifying assumptions. The remarkable part of our treatment will be that even with gross simplifications, the security question remains 'hard' in a technical sense.

We shall concentrate on the computer and operating system in making our first model.

In the accepted terminology, there are two (not disjoint) sets of entities which must be dealt with in the model. The first sort of entity is the _object_. It is enough to think of an object as any entity in the system which has a logically independent existence; a typical object may a terminal, a user, a program, a file, or the supervisory routine. An object is significant in that it has an identifiable name in the system and it may be operated upon by other objects. Of course, not every other object will be able to operate on a given object. Some objects, for example, are passive. By contrast, the programs which reside on files are _active_ entities. They read files, write files and call other programs. To distinguish these kinds of entities, we will call the active entities _subjects_. In a completely unprotected environment, a subject can access any object without restriction. Such a situation obviously raises havoc when users must be protected from each other. Therefore, a properly designed system should associate with a user, the set of capabilities which that user enjoys with respect to every other object. The emphasis is on the access to an object by a subject. Our goal is to arrive at a model which is rich enough to model actual systems but sufficiently restricted so that one can utilize mathematical techniques.

3.1.1 A Uniform Model of Protection. Our first task is to arrive at a model which is general but captures the essence of 'safety' from unauthorized access. Towards this end, let us assume that a computer contains a collection of abstract objects whose security is important. In practice, these objects would be interpreted as files containing important data. Let us furthermore postulate the existence of a 'reference monitor' which is to be interposed between a modern computer system with multiple users or even multiple processors. By assuming that all accesses to the protected objects go through the reference monitor, and further that all the hardware is infallible, one can model these systems by examining the dynamic behavior of the monitor. One should note that the effect of the users and of the operating system itself, are assumed to affect access to the objects only through the 'commands' which enter the monitor. The perfect hardware implements each access.

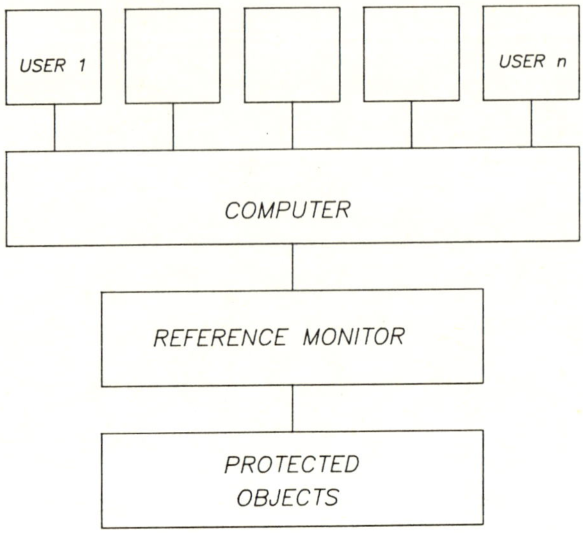

Figure 3.1
A computer system with a reference monitor.

A <u>protection system</u> consists of the following parts: a finite set of generic rights R, a finite set of commands of the form:

command $\alpha(X_1, X_2, \ldots, X_k)$

if $r_1 \in (X_{s_1}, X_{o_1}) \wedge$

$r_2 \in (X_{s_2}, X_{o_2}) \wedge$

...

$r_m \in (X_{s_m}, X_{o_m})$:

then

op_1

op_2

...

op_n

end

Or, if m is zero, simply

command $\alpha(X_1,X_2,\ldots,x_k)$

op_1

op_2

...

op_n

end

In our definition α is a name and $X_1,\ldots,X_k$ are formal parameters. Each op_i is one of the following primitive operations.

enter r **into** (X_s,X_o)

create subject X_s

create object X_o

delete r **from** (X_s,X_o)

destroy subject X_s

destroy object X_o

By convention $r,r_1,r_2,\ldots,r_k$ denote generic rights and $s,s_1,s_2,\ldots,s_m$ and $o,o_1,o_2,\ldots,o_m$ are integers between 1 and k. We also need to discuss the 'configurations' of a protection system. Intuitively, these correspond to the instantaneous configurations used in the usual definition of automata.

A <u>configuration</u> of a protection system is a triple (S,O,P), where S is the set of 'current subjects', O is the set of 'current objects', $S \subseteq O$, and P is an access matrix, which has a row for each subject in S and a column for each object in O, as shown in Figure 3.2. P[s,o] is a subset of R, the set of generic rights

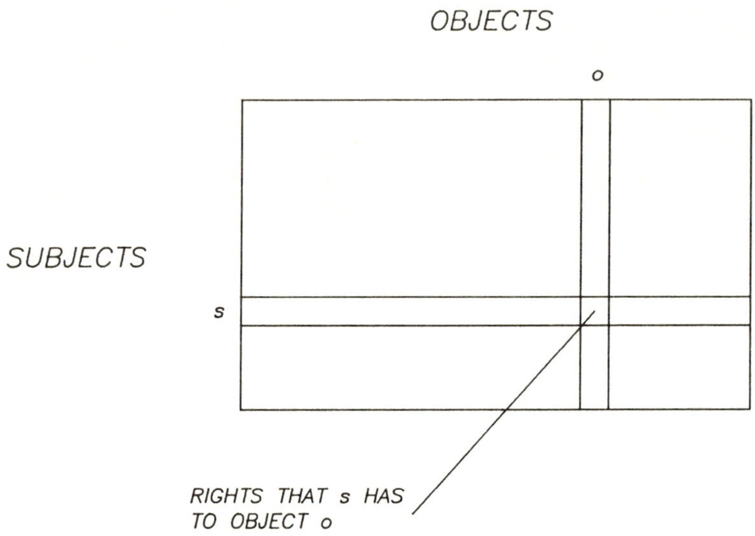

Figure 3.2
Access Matrix

Before proceeding further, let us consider a simple example which exposes the most common interpretation of the model.

We assume that each subject is a process and that the objects other than the subjects are files. Each file is owned by a process, and we shall model this notion by saying that the owner of the file has the right **own** to that file. The other generic rights are **read**, **write**, and **execute**. The allowable operations are as follows.

(1) A process may create a new file. The process which

creates the file has ownership of it. This may be represented by a procedure:

```
command CREATE(process,file)
     create object file
     enter own into(process,file)
end
```

(2) The owner of a file may confer any right to that file, other than **own**, on any subject (including the owner himself). We thus have three commands of the form:

```
command CONFER_r(owner,friend,file)
     if own ε (owner,file)
     enter r into (friend,file)
end
```

where r is **read**, **write**, or **execute**. Technically the r here is not a parameter but is used as an abbreviation for similar procedures.

(3) Similarly, we have three commands by which the ownership of a file may revoke another subject's access rights to the file.

```
command REMOVE_r(owner,exfriend,file)
     if own ε (owner,file) ∧
          r ε (exfriend,file)
     then delete r from (exfriend,file)
end
```

where r is **read**, **write**, or **execute**.

This completes the specification of most of the example protection system.

To formally describe the effect of the commands, we must give the rules for changing the state of the access matrix.

A typical access matrix is shown in Figure 3.2. Note that the s-th row may be thought of as a 'capability list' while the o-th column is an 'access-control list'.

Next, we need the rules for changing configurations in a protection system.

Let (S,O,P) and (S',O',P') be configurations of a protection system, and let op be one of the six primitive operations. We shall say that:

$$(S,O,P) \Rightarrow_{op} (S',O',P')$$

(which is read (S,O,P) *yields* (S',O',P') under op) if either:

1. op = **enter** r **into** (s,o) and S=S', O=O', $s \varepsilon S$, $o \varepsilon O$, $P'[s_1,o_1]=P[s_1,o_1]$ if $(s_1,o_1) \neq (s,o)$ and $P'[s,o]=P[s,o] \cup \{r\}$, or
2. op = **delete** r **from** (s,o) and S=S', O=O', $s \varepsilon S$, $o \varepsilon O$, $P'[s_1,o_1]=P[s_1,o_1]$ if $(s_1,o_1) \neq (s,o)$ and $P'[s,o]=P[s,o]-\{r\}$, or

3. op = **create subject** s', where s' is a new symbol not in O, $S'=S \cup \{s'\}$, $O'=O \cup \{s'\}$, $P'[s,o]=P[s,o]$ for all $(s,o) \in S \times O$, $P'[s,o]=\emptyset$ for all $o \in O'$, and $P'[s,s']=\emptyset$ for all $s \in S'$, or

4. op = **create object** o', where o' is a new symbol not in O, $S'=S$, $O'=O \cup \{o'\}$, $P'[s,o]=P[s,o]$ for all $(s,o) \in S \times O$, and $P'[s,o']=\emptyset$ for all $s \in S$, or

5. op = **destroy subject** s', where $s' \in S$, $S' = S - \{s'\}$, $O' = O - \{s'\}$, and $P'[s,o] = P[s,o]$ for all $(s,o) \in S' \times O'$, or

6. op = **destroy object** o', where $o' \in O - S$, $S'=S$, $O'=O - \{o'\}$, and $P'[s,o]=P[s,o]$ for all $(s,o) \in S' \times O'$.

Next we indicate how a protection system can execute a command. Let $Q = (S,O,P)$ be a configuration of a protection system containing:

command $\alpha(X_1, X_2, \ldots, X_k)$
    if $r_1 \in (X_{s_1}, X_{o_1}) \wedge$
        ...
    $r_m \in (X_{s_m}, X_{o_m})$
then
    op_1,
    op_2,
        ...
    op_n
end

Then we can say that

$$Q \mid\!-^{*}_{\alpha(x_1,\ldots,x_k)} Q'$$

where Q' is the configuration defined as follows:

1. If α's conditions are not satisfied, i.e. if there is some $1 \leq i \leq m$ such that r_i is not in $P[x_{s_i}, x_{s_i}]$, then Q = Q'.

2. Otherwise, i.e. if for all i between 1 and m, $r_i \in P[x_{s_i}, x_{s_i}]$, then let there exist configurations $Q_0, Q_1, \ldots, Q_n$ such that

$$Q = q_0 \Rightarrow^{*}_{op_1} Q_1 \Rightarrow^{*}_{op_2} \cdots \Rightarrow^{*}_{op_n} Q_n$$

where op_i^{*} denotes the primitive operation op_i with the actual parameters $x_1, \ldots, x_k$ replacing all occurrences of the formal parameters $X_1, \ldots, X_k$, respectively. Then Q' is Q_n.

We say that $Q \mid\!-_{\alpha} Q'$ if there exist parameters $x_1, \ldots, x_k$ such that we have $Q \mid\!-^{*}_{\alpha(x_1,\ldots x_k)} Q'$; we say $Q \mid\!- Q'$ if there exists a command α such that $Q \mid\!-_{\alpha} Q'$.

It is also convenient to write $Q \mid\!-^{*} Q'$, where $\mid\!-^{*}$ is the reflexive and transitive closure of $\mid\!-$. That is, $\mid\!-^{*}$ represents zero or more applications of $\mid\!-$.

Each command is given in terms of formal parameters. At

execution time, the formal parameters are replaced by actual parameters which are object names. Although the same symbols are often used in this exposition for formal and actual parameters, this should not cause confusion. The 'type checking' involved in determining that a command may be executed takes place with respect to actual parameters.

These protection systems compute like nondeterministic devices. This makes intuitive sense as the sequence of accesses of the protected objects may come in an unpredictable fashion.

The ability of the model to describe the policies used in real systems has been demonstrated in the literature.

It is important to be able to discuss safe (and hence unsafe) systems precisely. We shall approach the notion of 'safety' by attempting to characterize 'unsafety'. That, in turn, requires a definition of what it means for a command to 'leak' a right.

Given a protection system, we say command $\alpha(X_1, \ldots, X_k)$ <u>leaks generic right</u> r from configuration Q = (S,O,P) if α, when run on Q, can execute a primitive operation which enters r into a cell of the access matrix which did not previously contain r. More formally, there is some assignment of actual parameters $x_1, \ldots, x_k$ such that

1. $\alpha(x_1, \ldots, x_k)$ has its conditions satisfied in Q, i.e. for each clause '$r \in (X_i, X_j)$' in α's conditions we have $r \in P[x_i, x_j]$, and

2. if α's body is $op_1, \ldots, op_n$, then there exists an m, $1 \leq m \leq n$, and configurations $Q = Q_0, Q_1, \ldots, Q_{m-1} = (S', O', P')$, and $Q_m = (S'', O'', P'')$, such that

$$Q_0 \underset{op_1^*}{\Rightarrow} Q_1 \underset{op_2^*}{\Rightarrow} \cdots \underset{op_m^*}{\Rightarrow} Q_m$$

where op_i^* denotes op_i after substitution of $x_1, \ldots, x_k$ for $X_1, \ldots, X_k$ and there exists some s and o such that $r \notin P'[s,o]$ but $r \in P''[s,o]$. (Of course, op_m must be **enter r into (s,o)**).

Notice that given Q, α and r, it is easy to check whether α leaks r from Q even if α deletes r after entering it. This latter condition may seem unnatural but it is possible to arrange for a system to 'block' in the middle of a command and to interrupt a procedure.

It is important to note that leaks are not necessarily bad. The judgement about whether or not a leak is 'unfortunate' depends on whether or not the subjects are trusted.

Given a particular protection system and generic right r, we say that the initial configuration Q_0 is <u>unsafe</u> for r (or leaks r) if there is a configuration Q and a command α such that

1. $Q_0 \vdash^* Q$, and

2. α leaks r from Q.

We say that Q_0 is safe for r if Q_0 is not unsafe for r.

Now, let us pause a moment to examine what we have accomplished. We started with a concern about real security issues. A model was introduced which attempted to capture the ways in which objects might be accessed by processes. The model was progressively simplified until we now have a somewhat limited object of study. At least we have found a technically reasonably 'safety question' which we would like to solve. A solution could mean several different things. It would be nice to have a uniform procedure for solving any safety question for any protection system. If this is not possible, we could consider settling for a less general result.

If we were to derive an efficient algorithm for solving the safety question, it could be challenged on the grounds of the simplicity of the model, e.g. 'Has the problem been defined away?'. In fact, the results are somewhat surprising at first glance. It will be shown that there is no algorithm which can solve the safety question. Even in our restricted model, the problem is unsolvable which means that in any more realistic version, the same argument will carry over and the result will hold. In the next section, we shall summarize what is known about safety questions.

3.1.2 Some Theorems about Protection Systems. Now that we have a model, we will mention some of the results that are known about the safety question. First, the 'good news'. It is possible to find an algorithm to test for safety in such systems.

A protection system is _mono-operational_ if each command's

interpretation is a single primitive operation.

Theorem 1: There is an algorithm which decides whether or not a given mono-operational protection system and initial configuration is unsafe for a given generic right r.

The proof proceeds by analyzing computation sequences. Details of the proof may be found in the literature (See the Bibliographic Notes). It is not too difficult to solve this problem in polynomial time in the size of the initial matrix. On the other hand, a uniform solution when the commands are parameters of the problem makes the decision problem NP-complete.

Now let us consider general protection systems. Is it possible to solve the safety problem in a uniform manner for all protection systems? We are about to prove a negative result which becomes all the more significant because of the weakness of the model.

Theorem 2: It is undecidable whether a given configuration of a given protection system is safe for a given generic right.

Proof: There are a number of ways to prove this result. The access control matrix can be used to encode a string of potentially unbounded length on the main diagonal. If we have a Turing machine (a finite state device capable of scanning symbols α_i written on squares of an unbounded length tape, erasing and writing new symbols onto the squares, moving tape position one square to the left or right and changing states) as shown in Figure 3.3, we encode it into the matrix as shown in Figure 3.4.

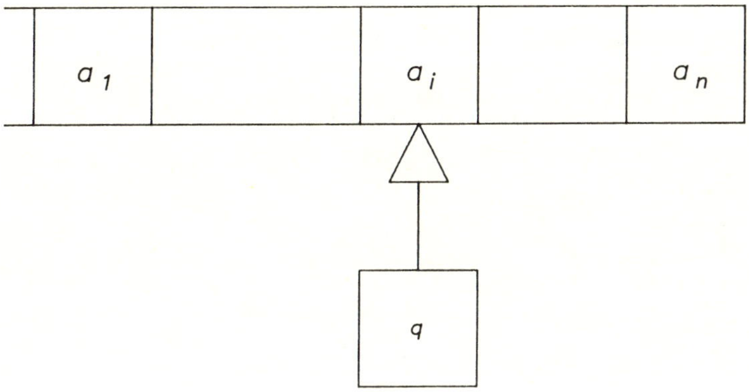

Figure 3.3
A Turing machine in state q reading α_i.

α_1	link				
	α_2	link			
		...	link		
			α_i, q	link	
				...	link
					α_n

Figure 3.4
Matrix which simulates machine in Fig. 3.3

To complete the proof, one must show how each move of the Turing machine can be accomplished by commands of the protection system. Moreover, the safety problem is solvable if and only if the Turing machine enters a designated final state. This last condition is unsolvable. The details of the construction are omitted here. Readers experienced with Turing machines or with machine-based complexity theory should now have a strong intuition about the class of theorems which hold.

While this result is discouraging from the point of view of guaranteeing safety, perhaps there are less general results to be obtained which are still valuable. Although Theorem 2 says that there is no single algorithm which can decide safety for all protection systems, one might hope that for each protection system, one could find a particular algorithm to decide safety. It can easily be seen that this is not possible. The simulation technique which was used previously can be applied to a universal Turing machine on an arbitrary input. This leads to a particular protection system for which it is undecidable whether a given initial configuration is safe for a given right. While we could give different algorithms to decide safety for different classes of systems there is no hope of covering all systems with a finite or even an infinite class of algorithms.

It might be the case that the power of these systems is caused by only one or two of the operations. It is natural to investigate the power of the fundamental operations. The first idea would be to limit the growth of such systems. While such a limitation of resources does make safety decidable, we can show the following.

Theorem 3: The question of safety for protection systems without **create** commands is complete in polynomial space.

Proof: A construction similar to Theorem 2 proves that any polynomial space bounded Turing machine can be reduced in polynomial time to an initial access matrix whose size is polynomial in the length of the Turing machine input.

Theorem 3 suggests that deciding safety for these systems probably requires exponential time.

The proof techniques which were employed above all make use of the diagonal of the access matrix in an essential way. What would happen if there were only a finite number of subjects and the number of objects which are not subjects was still unconstrained? Would the safety problem become 'tractable'?

Theorem 4: The safety problem for protection system with a finite number of subjects is decidable.

Moreover, it is shown that such protection systems are recursively equivalent to 'vector addition systems' and a connection between the safety question for the former and the covering problem for the latter is obtained. Although the safety question is decidable, it is again not something one would care to compute.

In an attempt to better understand wherein lies the computational power of protection systems, we shall now consider systems which can only increase in both size and in the entries in the matrix.

A protection system is monotonic if no command contains a primitive operation of the form

destroy subject s

destroy object o

delete r **from** (s,o)

A number of our colleagues who are familiar with operating systems constructs conjectured that monotonicity would reduce the computing power of protection systems. We shall show that it does not do so. It merely requires a different kind of proof which is more intricate and hence more interesting.

Theorem 5: It is undecidable whether a given configuration of a given monotonic protection system is safe for a given generic right.

Proof: The idea of the proof would be to encode an instance of the Post correspondence problem on the main diagonal of the access matrix. We would like to be able to grow an x-list and a y-list and at a suitable point in time, to compare them. Because of the monotonic restriction, the x and y lists must be 'interlaced' and the check for equality is done by 'pointer chasing'.

A study of previous proofs reveals that most of the commands have one or two conditions attached to them. It is necessary to use one command which requires five conditions. By using some coding tricks, these commands may be replaced by six commands each of which needs two conditions. This leads to the following.

Theorem 6: The safety question for monotonic protection systems is undecidable even when each command has at most two conditions.

Theorem 6 shows that the safety question for monotonic protection systems is undecidable, even if each command has at most two conditions. However, in many important practical situations, commands need only one condition. For example, a procedure for updating a file may only need to check that the user has the 'update' right to the file. In contrast to the undecidability of the cases discussed in the preceding section, the safety question is decidable if each command of a monotonic protection system has at most one condition.

A _mono-conditional_ protection system is one in which each command has at most one condition.

Mono-conditional protection systems are much more complicated than one might anticipate. It is still not known whether or not the safety problem is solvable for such systems.

We state without proof the best result known on this topic.

Theorem 7: Safety of mono-conditional protection systems with **create**, **enter**, and **delete** (but without **destroy**) commands is decidable.

3.1.3 Theories and Verifiability. In slightly different but more mathematical language, Theorem 2 can be restated as follows.

Theorem 8: The set of safe protection systems is not recursive.

We cannot, of course, also enumerate all safe systems, for a set is recursive if and only if both it and its complement are recursively enumerable. The bounded case, discussed in Theorem 3, is recursive though not computationally attractive.

Could we avoid the problems inherent in these results by shifting our perspective towards proving properties of the system in some particular formal language rather than dealing with algorithms directly?

To pursue this idea we shall say that a _formal language_ L is a recursive subset of the set of all strings over a given finite alphabet; the members of L are called _sentences_.

A _deductive theory_ T over a formal language L consists of a set A of axioms, where $A \subseteq L$, and a finite set of rules of inference which are recursive relations over L. The set of _theorems_ of T is defined inductively by:

1. if t is any axiom (i.e. if $t \in A$), then t is a theorem of T; and
2. if $t_1, \ldots, t_k$ are theorems of T and $(t_1, \ldots, t_k, t) \in R$ for some rule of inference R, then t is a theorem of T.

Thus, every theorem t of T has a _proof_ which is a finite sequence $(t_1,\ldots,t_n)$ of sentences such that $t = t_n$ and each t_i is either an axiom or follows from some subset of $t_1,\ldots,t_{i-1}$ by a rule of inference. We write T |- t to indicate that t is a theorem of T or is provable in T.

Two theories T and T' are said to be _equivalent_ if they have the same set of theorems though not necessarily the same axioms or rules of inference.

A theory T is _recursively axiomatizable_ if it has (or is equivalent to a theory with) a recursive set of axioms. The set of theorems of any recursively axiomatizable theory is _recursively enumerable_: we can generate all finite sequences of sentences, check each to see if it is a proof, and enter in the enumeration the final sentence of any sequence which is a proof. A theory T is _decidable_ if its theorems form a recursive set.

Since the set of safe protection systems is not recursively enumerable, it cannot be the set of theorems of a recursively axiomatizable theory. This means that the set of all safe protection systems cannot be generated effectively by rules of inference from a finite (or even recursive) set of safe systems. This does not rule out the possibility of effectively generating smaller, but still interesting, classes of safe systems. This observation can be refined, as we proceed to do, to establish further limitations on any recursively axiomatizable theory of protection.

A _representation of safety_ over a formal language L is an effective mapping $p \to t_p$ from protection systems to sentences.

We wish to interpret t_p as a statement of the safety of the protection system p. Therefore, we say that a theory T is <u>adequate</u> for proving safety if there is a representation $p \to t_p$ of safety such that $T \vdash t_p$ if and only if p is safe.

Analogs of the classic Church and Godel theorems for the undecidability and incompleteness of formal theories of arithmetic follow for formal theories of protection systems.

Theorem 10: Any theory T adequate for proving safety must be undecidable.

This theorem follows from Theorem 8 by noting that, were there an adequate decidable T, we could decide whether or not a protection system p was safe by checking whether or not $T \vdash t_p$.

Theorem 11: There is no recursively axiomatizable theory T which is adequate for proving safety.

This theorem follows from Theorems 8 and 9. If T were adequate and recursively axiomatizable, we could decide the safety of p by enumerating simultaneously the theorems of T and the set of unsafe systems; eventually, either t_p will appear in the list of theorems or p will appear in the list of unsafe systems, enabling us to decide the safety of p.

Theorem 11 shows that, given any recursively axiomatizable theory T and any representation $p \to t_p$ of safety, there is some protection system whose safety either is established incorrectly by T or is not established when it should be. This result in itself is of limited interest for two reasons: it is not constructive (i.e. it does not show how to find such a p); and, in practice, we may be willing to settle for inadequate theories as long as they are sound, that is as long as they do not err by falsely establishing the safety of unsafe systems. The next theorem overcomes the first limitation, showing how to construct a protection system p which is unsafe if and only if $T \vdash t_p$; the idea is to design the commands of p so that they can simulate a Turing machine that 'hunts' for a proof of the safety of p; if and when a sequence of commands finds such a proof, it generates a leak. If the theory T is sound, then such a protection system p must be safe but its safety cannot be provable in T.

A theory T together with a representation $p \to t_p$ of safety is <u>sound</u> if and only if p is safe whenever $T \vdash t_p$.

Theorem 12: Given any recursively axiomatizable theory T and any representation of safety in T, one can construct a protection system p for which $T \vdash t_p$ if and only if p is unsafe. Furthermore, if T is sound, then p must be safe, but its safety is not provable in T.

Proof: The proof of Theorem 2 shows how to define, given an indexing $\{M_i\}$ of Turing machines and an indexing $\{p_i\}$ of protection systems, a recursive function f such that

1. M_i halts if and only if $p_{f(i)}$ is unsafe.

Since T is recursively axiomatizable and the map $p \to t_p$ is computable, there is a recursive function g such that

2. $T \vdash t_{p_i}$ if and only if $M_{g(i)}$ halts;

the Turing machine $M_{g(i)}$ simply enumerates all theorems of T, halting if t_{p_i} is found. By the recursion theorem, one can effectively find an index j such that

3. M_j halts if and only if $M_{g(f(j))}$ halts.

Combining (1),(2), and (3), and letting $p = p_{f(j)}$, we get

4. $T \vdash t_p$ if and only if $M_{g(f(j))}$ halts,

if and only if M_j halts,

if and only if $p = p_{f(j)}$ is unsafe,

as was to be shown.

Now suppose that T is sound. Then t_p cannot be a theorem of T lest p be simultaneously safe by soundness and unsafe by (4). Hence $T \nvdash t_p$, and p is safe by (4).

The unprovability of the safety of a protection system p in a given sound theory T does not imply that the safety of P is unprovable in every theory. We can, for example, augment T by adding t_p to its axioms. However, Theorem 12 states that there will exist another safe p' whose safety is unprovable in the new theory T'. In other words, this abstract view shows that systems for proving safety are necessarily incomplete: no single effective deductive system can be used to settle all questions of safety.

The process of extending protection theories to encompass systems not provably safe in previous theories creates a progression of ever stronger deductive theories. With the stronger theories, proofs of safety can be shortened by unbounded amounts relative to weaker theories. This phenomena is known in logic and complexity theory.

Theorems 11 and 12 force us to settle for attempting to construct sound, but necessarily inadequate, theories of protection. What goals might we seek to achieve in constructing such a theory T? At the least, T should be nontrivial; theories that were sound because they had no theorems would be singularly uninteresting. We might also hope that the systems whose safety was provable in T, when added to the recursively enumerable set of unsafe systems, would form a recursive set. If this were so, then we could at least determine whether T were of any use in attempting to establish the safety or unsafety of a particular protection system p before beginning a search for a proof or disproof of the safety of P. The next theorem shows that this hope cannot be fulfilled.

Theorem 13: Given any recursively axiomatizable theory T and any sound representation of safety in T, the set

$$X = \{p \mid T \vdash t_p \text{ or } p \text{ unsafe}\}$$

is not recursive.

Proof: If X were recursive, then the safety of a protection system p could be decided as follows. First, we check to see if p is in X. If it is not, then it must be safe. If it is, then we enumerate simultaneously the theorems of T and the unsafe systems, stopping when we eventually find either a proof of p's safety or the fact that p is unsafe.

If we consider finite systems in which the number of objects cannot grow beyond the number present in the initial configuration, then the safety question becomes decidable, although any decision procedure is likely to require enormous amounts of time (cf. Theorem 3). This doubtless rules out practical mechanical safety test for these systems. However this does not rule out successful safety tests constructed by hand: ingenious or lucky people might be able to find proofs faster than any mechanical method. We show now that even this hope is ill-founded.

Although we can always obtain shorter safety proofs by choosing a proof system in which the rules of inference are more complicated, it makes little sense to employ proof systems whose rules are so complex that it is difficult to decide whether an alleged proof is valid. We shall regard a logical system as 'reasonable' if we can decide whether a given string of symbols constitutes a proof in the system in time which is a polynomial function of the string's length. Practical logical systems are reasonable by this definition. We show now that, corresponding to any reasonable proof system, there are protection systems which are bounded in size, but whose safety proofs or disproofs cannot be expected to have lengths bounded by polynomial functions of the size of the protection system. To do this we generalize the class **NP** to the class of problems which can be solved in polynomial <u>space</u>. **PSPACE** is the class of all problems which can be solved in polynomial space. It is known that any problem which can be solved nondeterministically in polynomial time is in **PSPACE**, but it is widely believed that **PSPACE** $\neq$ **NP**.

Theorem 14: For the class of protection systems in which the number of objects (hence, also, subjects) is bounded, safety (or unsafety) is polynomially verifiable by some reasonable logical system if and only if **PSPACE** = **NP**, that is, if and only if any problem solvable in polynomial space is solvable in polynomial time.

Proof: By Theorem 3, the safety and unsafety problems for systems of bounded size are both in **PSPACE**. Hence, if **PSPACE** = **NP**, then there would be **NP**-time Turing machines to decide both safety and unsafety. Given such machines, we could define a reasonable logical system in which safety and unsafety were polynomially verifiable: the 'axioms' would correspond to the initial configurations of the Turing machines and the 'rules of inference' to the transition tables from the machines.

Also by Theorem 3, any problem in **PSPACE** is reducible to a question concerning the safety (or unsafety) of a protection system whose size is bounded by a polynomial function of the size of the original problem. Now if the safety (or unsafety) of protection systems with bounded size were polynomial verifiable, we could decide safety (or unsafety) in NP-time by first 'guessing' a proof and then verifying that it was a proof (performing both tasks in polynomial time). By Theorem 3, we could then solve any problem in **PSPACE** in **NP**-time, showing that **PSPACE** = **NP**.

Since the above result applies equally to proofs of safety and unsafety, one must expect that there are systems for which it will be just as difficult and costly to penetrate the system as to prove that it can (or cannot) be done. In mono-operational systems, however, the situation is quite different.

Theorem 15: The safety of mono-operational system is polynomially verifiable.

Proof: This result follows from Theorem 1 whose proof shows that the unsafety question of mono-operational systems is solvable in NP-time. Although we simply observe that to demonstrate unsafety, one need only exhibit a command sequence leading to a leak. It can be shown that there are short unsafe command sequences if any exist at all: an upper bound on the length of such sequences is $g(m+1)(n+1)$, where g is the number of generic rights, m the number of subjects and n the number of objects. Thus an unsafe sequence (if it exists) has a length bounded by a polynomial function of the system size.

By Theorems 3 and 15, proofs of unsafety for mono-operational systems are short, but the time to find the proofs cannot be guaranteed to be short; at the worst we might have to enumerate each of the sequences of length at most g(m+1)(n+1) that could produce a leak. However, while proofs of unsafety are short for mono-operational systems, proofs of safety are not.

Theorem 16: For mono-operational systems, safety is polynomial verifiable if and only if **NP** is closed under complementation.

Proof: If **NP** were closed under complement, then safety would be in **NP** because unsafety is in **NP** by Theorem 14. Thus there would be a nondeterministic Turing machine for checking safety in polynomial time, which would demonstrate that safety is polynomial verifiable.

Conversely, suppose that safety were polynomially verifiable. We could then construct a nondeterministic Turing machine which would guess a proof of safety and then check it in polynomial time, hence safety would be in **NP**. But unsafety is in **NP** in Theorem 14 and if any **NP** complete problem has its complement in **NP**, then **NP** is closed under complement.

These results imply that system penetrators have a slight advantage when challenging mono-operational systems: any system that can be penetrated has a short command sequence for doing so. However, it may still take enormous amounts of time to find such sequences, as no systematic method of finding an unsafe command sequence in polynomially bounded time is likely to be found.

3.1.4 A Decidable Model. The results of the preceding sections support skepticism toward proving systems safe, for there is no single, systematic, general approach to establishing the safety or unsafety of arbitrary protection systems. Hence we are forced to deal with approaches that are less general, or attack the problem from a different point of view. There are several possible approaches to take.

Despite the undecidability and intractability results, we can still try to prove particular protection systems safe. After all, the incompleteness, undecidability, and intractability results in number theory have not stopped mathematicians from trying to prove interesting theorems, and so our results for protection systems should not stop us from trying to prove the safety of interesting protection systems. Our results merely stand as a warning that proving systems safe is not likely to be easy.

Rather than trying to guarantee the safety of a protection system, which might be expensive, we might instead seek to give shorter demonstrations that the system is 'probably safe' or 'safe beyond a reasonable doubt'. One possible approach might be to construct theories of protection which occasionally, though with very low probability, produced a 'proof' that an unsafe system was safe.

Recognizing the well-known fact that certain access paths may well be too expensive to eliminate, we might concentrate on trying to prove that any way of compromising a given protection system must likewise be too expensive. Given this approach, the question of central importance would not be whether we could prove that a system is safe, but whether we could prove that finding a breach of security is, say, **NP**-hard or even harder.

Perhaps the best approach would be to develop techniques for proving the safety of sufficiently simple protection systems. We now investigate a class of systems which possesses a linear time algorithm for deciding safety. These models are at the opposite end of the spectrum of operating systems models. Because they are less general, their expressability is of concern. We will attempt to explain their properties briefly here.

The basic idea is to use a type of dynamically changing labeled directed graph as the model. The nodes of the graph represent 'users' and the labels on a directed arc are some nonempty subset of {r,w,c} where r stands for 'read', w for 'write' and c for 'call'. Formally, the model consists of a finite directed graph with no self-loops and each branch labeled as above. We write each explicit right as an arc label. Therefore, a label r on an arc from x to y means that there is a set of rights γ on an arc from x to y and $r \in \gamma$. Each graph may be transformed by any of the five rewriting rules.

> **Take:** Let x,y, and z be three distinct vertices in a protection graph, and let there be an arc from x to y with label γ such that $r \in \gamma$ and an arc from y to z with some label $\alpha \subseteq \{r,w,c\}$. The **take** rule allows one to add the arc from x to z with label α, yielding a new graph G'. Intuitively, x takes the ability to do α to z from y. We represent this as

shown below:

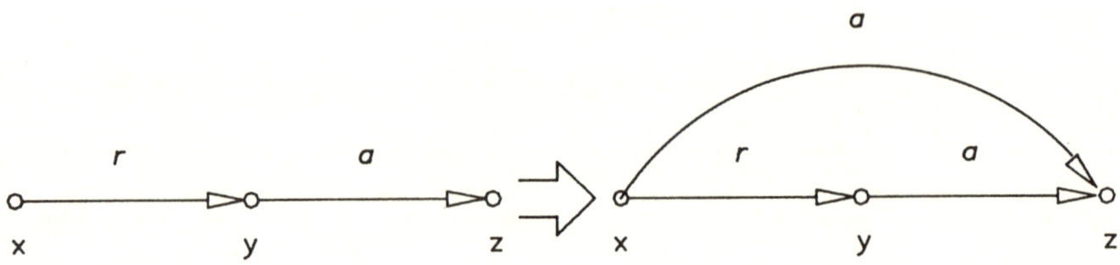

Grant: Let x,y, and z be three distinct vertices in a protection graph G, and let there be an arc from x to y with label γ such that $w \in \gamma$ and an arc from x to z with label $\gamma \subseteq \{r,w,c\}$. The **grant** rule allows one to add an arc from y to z with label α, yielding a new graph G′. Intuitively, x grants y the ability to do α to z. In our representation:

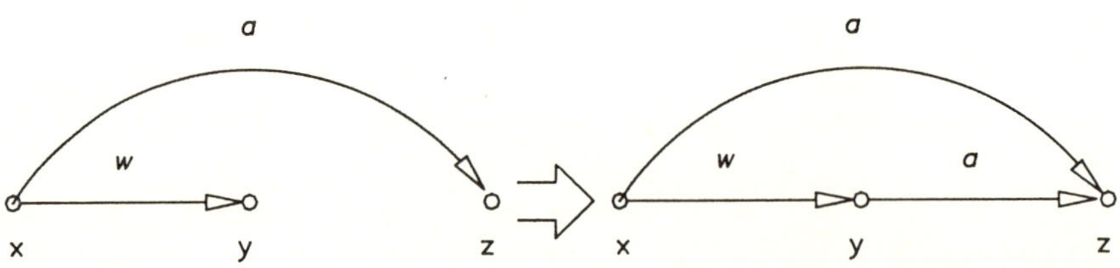

Create: Let x be any vertex in a protection graph; the **create** operation allows one to add a new vertex n and an arc from x to n with label {r,w,c}, yielding a new graph G′. Intuitively, x creates a new user that it can read, write, and call. In our representation

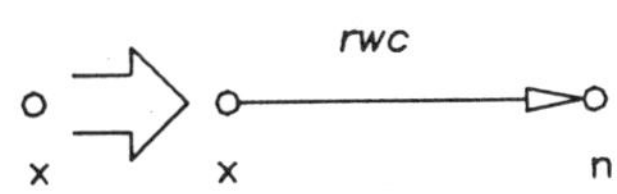

Call: Let x,y and z be distinct vertices in a protection graph G, and let $\alpha \subseteq \{r,w,c\}$ be the label on an arc from x to y and γ the label on an arc from x to z such that $c \in \gamma$. The **call** rule allows one to add a new vertex n, an arc from n to y with label α, and an arc from n to z with label r, yielding a new graph G'. Intuitively x is calling a program z and passing parameters y. The 'process' is created to effect the call: n can read the program z and α can read the parameters. In our representation:

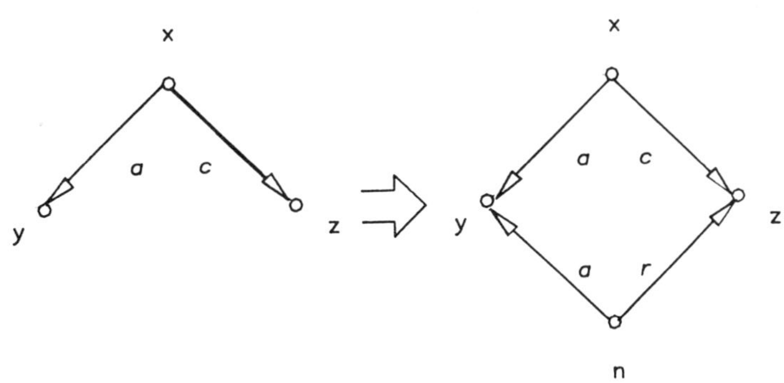

Remove: Let x and y be distinct vertices in a protection graph G with an arc from x to y with label α. The **remove** rule allows one to remove the arc from x to y, yielding a new graph G$'$. Intuitively, x removes its rights to y. In our representation

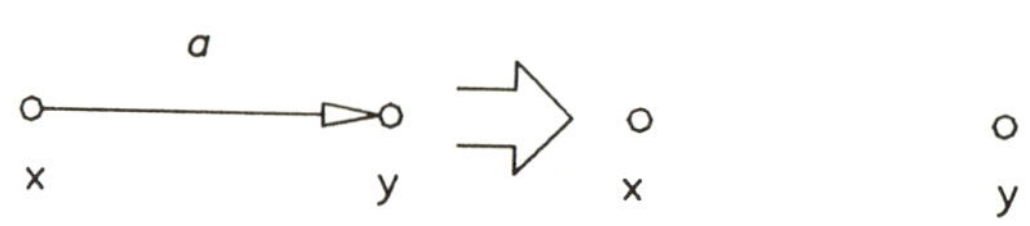

The **remove** rule is defined mainly for completeness, since real protection systems tend to have such a rule.

The operation of applying one of the rules to a protection graph G yielding a new protection graph G$'$ is written $G \vdash G'$. As usual, $G \vdash^* G'$ denotes the reflexive, transitive closure of $\vdash$.

An important technical point is that this is monotone in the sense that if a rule can be applied, then adding arcs cannot change this.

The basic application of this model is to answer questions of the form: "Can p α q?" where $\alpha \in \{r,w,c\}$. As an example, we shall show that if x can **call** y then x can read y. This is just the kind of property we wish to deduce from such a model since the fact that x can read y may have been an unintentional consequence of allowing x to call y.

Fact 1: In a protection graph G

Proof: Apply the following rules.

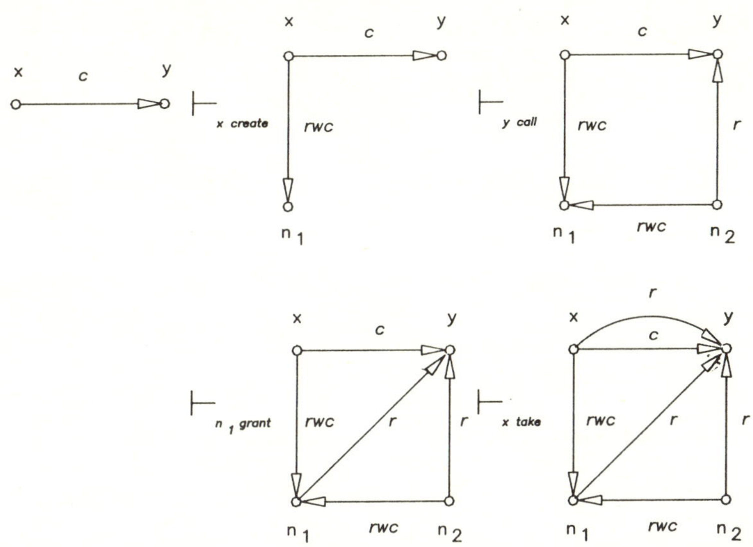

The present model is very restricted. Unlike the model in previous sections which was uniform with respect to many problems, the present model is quite specialized and was selected from the literature because of its previous occurrence in practice.

It is worth discussing what the technical results are in this case. It can be shown that there are two simple conditions that are necessary and sufficient to determine if vertex p can α vertex q. Let G be a protection graph and $\alpha \in \{r,w,c\}$. Call p and q connected if there exists a path between p and q independent of orientation or labels of the arcs. Define the predicates:

Condition 1: p and q are connected in G.

Condition 2: There exists a vertex x in G and an arc from x to q with label β such that $\alpha = r$ implies $\{r,c\}\ \beta \neq \emptyset$, or $\alpha = w$ implies $w \in \beta$, or $\alpha = c$ implies $c \in \beta$.

Informally, these conditions state that p can α q if and only if there is an undirected path between p and q (condition 1) and some vertex x α's q (condition 2).

It is not hard to see that conditions 1 and 2 are necessary. By a sequence of lemmas, quite similar to the previous example, sufficiency can be established. One can draw the following inferences.

Theorem 17: Let p and q be distinct vertices in a protection graph and α a label. Conditions 1 and 2 are necessary and sufficient to imply p can α q. The consequence of the main theorem is that the protection policy for this **take-grant** system can be precisely stated.

Policy: If p can read (**write, call**) q, then any user in the connected component containing p and q can attain the right to **read**, **write**, and **call** q.

This policy may appear to be more undiscriminating than one might have expected. A primary reason for this is that the **take-grant** system treats all elements of the system the same whereas most protection models recognize two different entities: subjects and objects. If we dichotomize the vertices of our model into subject and object sets and require (as is usually the case) that only subjects can initiate the application of our rules, then the system becomes much more difficult to analyze. Such an analysis has been carried out. It should be noted that in the dichtomized model there are protection graphs that satisfy conditions 1 and 2 for which p can α q is false. There has been additional work in extending this model to handle progressively more complex cases.

3.2 Multilevel Security. There have been many attempts to use access control methods to encompass a broad range of security issues. For instance, attaching the capabilities to the subjects and requiring no subject to execute outside his specified capabilities implements the "principle of least privilege" which *confines* the potential damage of a subject's actions to that locality specified by his capability list. Attaching capabilities to subjects also admits an efficient implementation of access control methods. The technique of *capability-based addressing* associates the capabilities of a program with the addresses of segments, and accesses to data objects are always mediated by a process that does not allow access violations.

Although many famous security threats are met by access controls (e.g., access-controls meet the Trojan horse threat by requiring each program to execute only in a manner consistent with its capabiliites, so that a user program cannot execute in supervisor mode because its capabilities are not extensive enough to access its own runtime fields) they do not deal effectively with the central problem of *multilevel* security; that is, ensuring that undesirable information *flow* does not take place.

Figure 3.5 illustrates the generalized security problem in which a subject s creates an object o which operates within a specified environment or resource. Since the owner of the resource may be a subject to which s is accountable, the actions of s may have far-reaching consequences for the overall security state of the system.

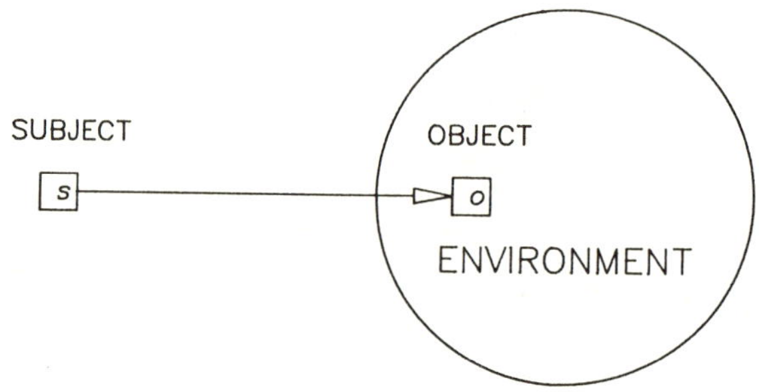

Figure 3.5
Generalized Security Threat

We have already described how various models can be applied to attempt to insure that o cannot access s's files illegally or to insure that o is protected from intrusion by s, but we have not yet dealt effectively with the situation in which o may be used as a _transmitter_ of information. There are many channels through which o can "leak" information that s wants to keep secret. We will assume that o is owned by an enemy subject from whom the information that s passes to o is to be kept secret.

1. o may hold the sensitive data in memory, releasing it to the enemy at a later time;
2. o may write information directly into the enemy's file;
3. o may create its own file and grant the enemy access to the file;
4. o may send messages to a process 'owned' by the enemy;
5. if s is "billed" for using the environment, o may encode information in the bill;
6. o may use system interlocks as boolean variables (0 = unlocked, 1 = locked) to send bits to the enemy;
7. o may alter its performance characteristics to signal the enemy.

It is usual to classify these and other channels through which information may flow in a software system as _storage_(1,2), _legitimate_ (3,4), _covert_ (5,6,7) channels.

By far the greatest effort has been placed in handling the many legitimate channels for leakage that exist in a large software system. This problem has been called the _confinement problem_, and there have been many policies suggested for confining programs. One possibility is to isolate a program, disallowing the confined program from making any calls on other programs. A relaxed form of isolation is the policy of transitivity: if a program s calls an object o, then either o is "trusted" or o is itself confined.

The most widely adopted approach to the multilevel problem has been through the use of security <u>kernels</u>, that is, small, tightly constrained operating systems that deliver secure services to users by implementing system procedures which have been protected against system threats or by calling other software which has been previously identified as <u>trusted</u>. Figure 3.6 illustrates the subject/object/access configuration of a secure operating system using kernel.

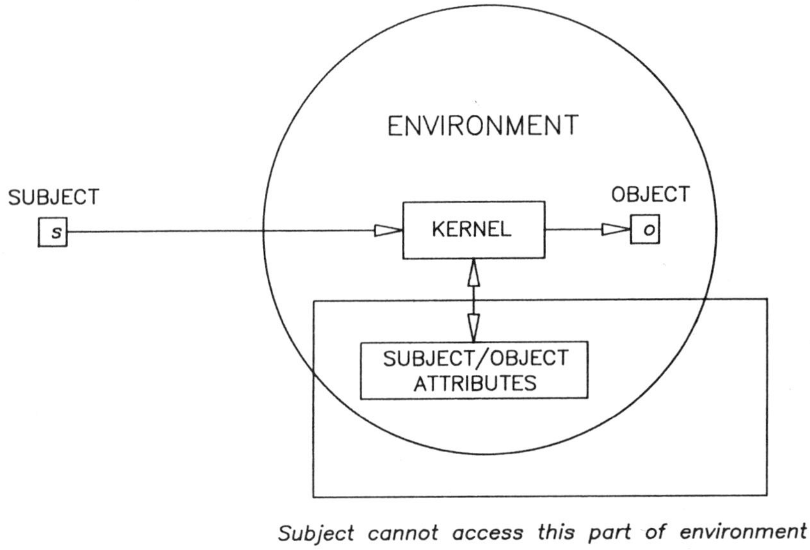

Figure 3.6
Subject/Object Access Through Kernel

The principal model on which current kernelized operating systems are constructed is the Bell and LaPadula model. In its broad outlines, the model is fairly simple. The multilevel system assigns security levels and integrity levels to each system object. A security level is specified by an ordered pair (x,y), where x is an authorization level (e.g., secret, top secret, etc.)

and y is a set of compartments (e.g., restricted, crypto). The usual situation is that the authorizations are linearly ordered and a partial ordering on the security levels is determined by the following condition:

$$(u,v) \leq (x,y) \text{ iff } u \leq x \text{ and } v \subseteq y.$$

The notion of integrity level is entirely analogous to that of security level. In general, one is given a set of levels $s_1,\ldots,s_n$ and a partial ordering on them. The operating system must allow reading and writing of information in the obvious directions between lower levels and higher levels in such a way that information can never flow from a high level to a lower level.

Early attempts at satisfying these conditions lead to so-called "highwatermark" systems in which access to classified documents by lower levels resulted in the reclassifying upwards of the documents -- leading, of course, to overclassification of documents. The Bell and LaPadula model attempts to satisfy these conditions by specifying two properties for each of the security and integrity problems.

The *-property: Writing is permitted only into an object with $\geq$ ($\leq$) the writer's security (integrity) level.

The Simple Security Condition: Reading is permitted only from an object with $\leq$ ($\geq$) the reader's security (integrity) level.

The security kernel is the authority whose responsibility it is to mediate the Bell and LaPadula model of multilevel security.

There have been a variety of attempts to produce working kernelized operating systems.

3.3 Databases and Inference. The interconnection between the gathering of data and the computer dates from the invention of the punched card which made it possible to complete the 1890 census within a decade. The 1980 census tabulations were available within six months after the completion of the census thanks to a century of advancements in our ability to collect and process data. This mode of information storage, however, gives rise to security problems of types unknown in the nineteenth century. In particular, the security measures to be discussed here were unnecessary, yet today security and integrity are major concerns. The purpose of this section is to discuss the inference mechanisms through which it is possible to extract information from statistical databases. This is the prototypical compromise problem for stored information. The underlying issues revolve around finding a method to satisfy the conflicting needs for statistical information about segments of society and the rights of the individual to privacy. The collection and analysis of data has long been a research tool in the social sciences, and few people would argue with the need for maintaining information from which general trends can be observed. On the other hand, it is quite easy to create scenarios in which the existence of large-scale databases containing information about individuals can be misused. In fact, just such abuse has been reported of a public agency's database, while a recent report of the General Accounting Office noted a number of weaknesses in the databases of the Social Security Administration.

To strike a balance, the Census Bureau of the United States does not issue its raw data, but rather makes available census tracts which are designed to give statistical information without providing information about individuals. And, because of the magnitude of the census information, individual privacy appears to be insured, simply because individuals are "lost" in the masses of data.

Such intuitions are not always correct. In the sequel, we will present a simple model of databases and the storage of information within them. This model will be used to address the issues involved in releasing information without compromising individual privacy. The questions involved will be reduced to simple combinatorial problems concerning the underlying models. While the model presented here is an abstraction of the security situation as it occurs in practice, our results appear to remain valid even when the simplifying assumptions are considerably weakened.

3.3.1 Databases. We will assume that a database is presented as an array of information. Rows of the array represent individuals and columns represent information classifications.

Consider, for example, the following database.

Person	Sex	Field	Location	Age	Salary
Alpha	M	Algebra	East	34	x_1
Beta	M	Topology	West	29	x_2
Gamma	M	Logic	South	54	x_3
Delta	F	Appl. Math	East	45	x_4
Epsilon	M	Geometry	West	48	x_5
Zeta	F	Logic	East	23	x_6
Eta	F	Algebra	South	66	x_7
Theta	M	Topology	South	58	x_8
Iota	F	Geometry	South	33	x_9
Kappa	F	Appl. Math	North	27	x_{10}
Lambda	M	Appl. Math	West	33	x_{11}

Figure 3.7
Sample Data Base

For simplicity, we will consider databases in this form rather than resort to the more complex representations which faithfully model implementation detail, but obscure structure. It is sufficient to note that the results we will quote below extend to the more realistic models in an entirely straightforward way.

Information about individuals represented in a database will be obtained by answers to <u>queries</u> about subpopulations. A subpopulation consists of all individuals having particular values or ranges of values for a given set of characteristics. Subpopulations may also be combined with union and intersection operations in the obvious ways. For example, the following are valid subpopulations of our sample database:

topologists

females from the south or east

males between the ages of 30 and 50.

There are two types of statistical queries about subpopulations. We can either ask for a count of the subpopulation or for statistics regarding some characteristics of the subpopulation. For example, valid query responses include the following:

The median salary of topologists

The number of mathematicians from the east

The largest salary of women mathematicians

The average salary of women topologists and male logicians

Queries are assumed to be the legitimate queries necessary for statistical studies of the given population and, as such, it is desirable to provide usable answers in all cases. Conversely, the individuals represented by the information in the database have been insured of the confidentiality of their personal data. We will say that the database has been _compromised_ when this confidentiality is violated. A compromise involves determining information which is regarded as hidden in the database. This hidden information may consist of actual values (e.g., salaries) or bivalent information (e.g., has been arrested). Among the mathematical questions which are natural to ask about such a concept are those which characterize the _complexity_ of compromise under varying query types. The motivation for studying the complexity of compromise is much the same as for studying the cryptocomplexity of enciphering schemes. Our complexity measure for database security is a simple count of the number of distinct queries needed to compromise the database in various settings. In the sequel, we will address different aspects of these problems.

The model presented here does not give an exact representation of "real" database problems. As we mentioned above, we do not work with the *relational model* of databases but rather with a simpler array model. This assumption has little effect on the translation of results to the relational model, since the constraints on the systems which permit compromise turn out to be similar. We often assume that *any* group of k people can be grouped together into a query, which is often not the case. If, however, compromise is not possible when such capability is permitted, then it surely is not possible when it is denied. Such assumptions are sometimes balanced by simplifying assumptions which *restrict* the user; we may, for example, restrict the *overlap* between pairs of queries. It may in principle be possible to form two queries

$$\text{AVERAGE}\{x_1, x_2, \ldots, x_n\}$$

$$\text{AVERAGE}\{x_1, x_2, \ldots, x_n, x_{n+1}\}$$

from which the value of x_{n+1} is easily found. Finally, the potential penetrator of a database always brings with him a store of *a priori* knowledge which he can use in making inferences about protected information. In practice, the assumptions made here tend to be overly restrictive, therefore a statement of the form

"The database may be compromised in k queries of type..."

tends to be an accurate portrayal of a system weakness, while a statement of the form

"No fewer than k queries will compromise the database"

might provide a lower bound which is not too high in practice.

3.3.2. Compromise by Varying Query Types. We consider methods of database compromise under varying sets of queries. We begin with the situation in which AVERAGE queries are permitted with restrictions on the size of the query set and the overlap between pairs of queries. In this case there are tight bounds on the number of queries needed to compromise. These results are established by linear independence and matrix inversion techniques. Next, we turn to the case of MEDIAN queries and, by using complex forms of binary splitting techniques are able to establish nearly matching bounds. Finally, we consider instances of data distortion in order to determine the ultimate limits on security in the case where we attempt to insure security by greatly restricting the allowable query types. Tight bounds are established by finite geometric arguments.

3.3.3. Linear Queries. Perhaps the most natural setting for the query problem is the one in which the database is simply a set of values $x_1,\ldots,x_n$ so that queries are determined by an index set I. A response to an I-query might be

$$(1/|I|) \sum_{i \in I} x_i$$

If all possible query sets I are allowed, then compromise is trivial. The simplest compromise is achieved by letting $|I|=1$.

Another possibility is to let

$$J = I \cup \{x_k\}, \; x_k \notin I.$$

A priori knowledge may also lead to trivial solutions. For instance, if the x_i's represent salaries, a user will know certainly his own salary and possibly the salaries of a few colleagues.

The following complexity measure takes such considerations into account. Define $S(n,k,r,m)$ to be the minimum number of queries needed to compromise a database of n elements where each query involves exactly k individuals, no pair of queries overlaps in more than r positions and at most m values are known in advance.

To set ideas, we show that $S(4,3,2,0) \leq 4$. To see this, consider the queries

$$Q_1 = x_1+x_2+x_3$$
$$Q_2 = x_1+x_2+x_4$$
$$Q_3 = x_1+x_3+x_4$$
$$Q_4 = x_2+x_3+x_4.$$

It follows that

$$x_4 = (-2Q_1+Q_2+Q_3+Q_4)/3.$$

A simple argument shows that this is optimal; i.e., $S(4,3,2,0)=4$.

One property of the S function is that it reveals that small databases can be secured by insisting on large queries. That is, $S(n,k,r,m) = \infty$ if

$$n < k^2/2r+k/2+(m+1)/2-(m+1)^2/2r.$$

To prove this, assume that a set of queries has been proposed from which the database can be compromised. Without loss of generality, let the first query be

$$x_1+x_2+x_k.$$

Now, there must be at least $(k-m-1)/r$ further queries, since some linear combinations of the queries can be reduced to a linear combination of at most $(m+1)$ x_i, k x_i were introduced in the first query and overlap between the queries is limited to r. Furthermore, the second query must introduce at least k-r new elements of the database, the third at least k-2r, and so on. Thus, the number of elements in the database must be at least

$$k + \sum_{i=1}^{(k-m-1)/r} (k-ir)$$

from which the result follows.

The query sequence in the proof given above can be restricted further by observing that not only must all m+1 database elements of the first query appear again, but the linear combination of queries used to compromise must involve positive and negative coefficients to insure the proper cancellation. Careful application of this argument can be used to achieve the following lower bound on S:

$$S(n,k,r,m) \geq (2k-(m+1))/r.$$

The bound is obtained as follows. We assume that $x_1, \ldots, x_m$ are known in advance and that x_{m+1} is determined after t queries. We represent the query Q_i by

$$Q_i = \sum_{j=1}^{k} d_{m_{ij}} x_i, \quad i=1,\ldots,t,$$

where,

$$1 \leq m_{i1} \leq \ldots \leq m_{ik} \leq n,$$

for $1 \leq i \leq t$, and

$$|\{m_{i1},\ldots,m_{ik}\} \cap \{m_{j1},\ldots,m_{jk}\}| \leq r,$$

for $i \neq j$.

Because t queries suffice to determine x_{m+1}, we have

$$\sum_{j=1}^{m+1} b_j x_j = \sum_{i=1}^{t} a_i Q_i = \sum_{s=1}^{n} \sum_{i=1}^{t} a_i d_{is} x_s$$

where $b_{m+1} \neq 0$, $a_i \neq 0$, for all $i=1,\ldots,t$, and d_{is} is the characteristic function for x_s in Q_i. We now extend the above observation by noticing that at most m+1 of the terms in

$$\sum_{i=1}^{t} a_i \; d_{is}$$

are nonzero. We assume that each x_t is used in some query, so that the kth such term is zero iff there are i,j such that d_{it} and d_{jt} are nonzero and a_i and a_j have opposite signs.

We now use this fact to prove the lower bound. Choose two queries which appear with opposite signs and assume that they have V values in common. Let K1 and K2 represent the number of known values among the remaining k-V. The (k-(V+K1))/r queries are needed to cancel the remaining terms in the first query, and (k-(V+K2))/r are needed for the second query. Since V $\leq$ r and K1+K2 $\leq$ m+1, we have the claimed bound.

Furthermore, matching the upper and lower bounds is possible in many cases:

1. $S(n,k,1,0) = 2k-1$, if $n \geq k^2-k+1$,

2. $S(n,k,1,1) = 2k-2$, if $n \geq (k-1)^2+2$

3. $S(n,kr+a,r,2a-1) = 2k$, if $n \geq k^2r+2a$.

In each of these cases, a constructive derivation is possible. For (1), the queries used are

$$Q_i = \sum_{j=1}^{k} x_{k(i-1)+j}, \quad i=1,\ldots,k-1,$$

$$Q_{k+i-1} = x_{k^2+k+1} + \sum_{j=1}^{k-1} x_{k(j-1)+i},$$

for $i=1,\ldots,k$, with

$$(1/k)\left(\sum_{i=0}^{k-1} Q_{k+i} - \sum_{i=1}^{k-1} Q_i\right) = x_{k^2-k+1}$$

For (2), the queries used are:

$$Q_i = x_1 + \sum_{j=2}^{k} x_{(k-1)(i-1)+j}, \quad i=1,\ldots,k-1,$$

$$Q_{k+i-1} = x_{(k-1)^2+2} + \sum_{j=1}^{k-1} x_{(k-1)(j-1)+i+1}, \quad 1 \leq i \leq k-1$$

with

$$(1/k-1)\left(\sum_{i=1}^{k-1} Q_i - Q_{k-1+i}\right) = x_1 - x_{2+(k-1)^2}$$

so that $x_{2+(k-1)^2}$ is determined by x_1.

For (3), the queries used are:

$$Q_i = \sum_{j=1}^{kr} x_{kr(i-1)+j} + \sum_{m=1}^{a} x_{m+rk^2},$$

$$Q_{k+i} = \sum_{j=1}^{kr} \sum_{m=1}^{r} x_{kr(j-m)+(i-m)r+1} + \sum_{p=1}^{a} x_{a+p+rk^2}$$

where in both cases $i=1,\ldots,k$, and

$$\sum_{i=1}^{k} (Q_i - Q_{k+i}) = k \sum_{m=1}^{a} (x_{m+rk^2} - x_{a+m+rk^2}).$$

so that if 2a-1 of the values on the right are known, the last one can be computed.

From (3) we see that if the overlap is fixed and at least one element is known the optimal method is determined for infinitely many query sizes. Gaps between the best known upper and lower bounds occur when the allowed overlap grows at a rate proportional to the query size.

Further extensions of this model have dealt with the case in which queries are not restricted to size k, but can have any size in the ranges [k,n-1] and to the case in which answers are given as weighted sums rather than as averages. In this latter case, if the weights are unknown and if no information is available *a priori*, then the database cannot be compromised by the methods described here. However, if even one value is known, total compromise is possible. This suggests that if a conspirator is able to add information concerning himself to the database, he can compromise a previously secure system.

3.3.3. Median Queries. The median is often used as a statistic in place of the mean because of the many well-known situations in which it provides more realistic information about a sample. Therefore an important query type involves medians, or more generally, any query which returns *exact* values from the database. The model is exactly as in the pevious section, except that the AVERAGE query is replaced by MEDIAN: a typical query specifies an index set I and requests

$\{x_i \mid i \in I\}$.

Many security properties change when medians are allowed. Since the response to a median query is exact (that is, it corresponds to an actual entry), we need only assume that all entries are distinct to devise a trivial compromise algorithm: if two overlap 1 queries return the same result the database has been compromised since there is no ambiguity about the owner of the returned value. Furthermore, changing individual values in a median query need not affect the response to that query. For example, any value larger than the true median can be assumed to be $+\infty$. Thus, we know immediately that if queries are size k or larger, the top k/2 and bottom k/2 values in the database can never be determined. In addition, some values are apparently easier to determine than others: it is easier to extract the values _near_ the median of the database than to determine extreme values. We will shortly connect these observations with a more general class of combinatorial problems.

Let us first make the assumption that all database elements are distinct. This assumption, while not justified in practice, is not unreasonable when one is working with a small random sample of a large database. After stating some results in this restricted model we will show how to remove some of the restrictions.

There are some simple methods of compromise in the best case. Two median queries with overlap 1 and which return the same value compromise the database, but if entries are not unique and unlimited overlap is not allowed, there is still a possibility for compromise by the three queries:

Q_1: $\mathrm{MEDIAN}\{x_1, x_2, \ldots, x_k\} = a$

Q_2: $\mathrm{MEDIAN}\{x_{k+1}, x_2, \ldots, x_k\} = b$

Q_3: $\mathrm{MEDIAN}\{x_{k+2}, x_2, \ldots, x_k\} = c.$

We may assume that $c>a>b$. Then Q_1 and Q_2 imply that $x_{k+1} < a \leq x_1$ and Q_1 and Q_3 imply that $x_{k+2} > a \geq x_1$. Hence, $a \geq x_1 \geq a$, so that $x_1 = a$. Notice that this is the best case since if $a=b$ or $a=c$, then x_1 cannot be determined in this way.

In the worst case, it is possible to show that $O(\log k)$ median queries of length k are required to compromise a database of n elements. The proof involves information theoretic arguments. The best known upper bound is $O(\log^2 k)$ queries. The algorithm involves applying binary search techniques to derive balanced sets from which a median element can be found to match a known median value. For simplicity we prove here the weaker $3k/2 + 7/2$ bound for median queries of size k in a database of $n \geq k+2$ elements. First, compute the medians of all k-sized subsets of $\{x_1, \ldots, x_{k+1}\}$. These queries lead to exactly two values, say h and m. These medians define two sets H and L with $|H| = |L| = (k+1)/2$, where:

$H=\{x_i \mid x_i \leq h\}$

$L=\{x_i \mid x_i \geq m\}$

The sets are determined by noting that $x_i \in H$ iff the median of $\{x_1, \ldots, x_{k+1}\}-\{x_i\}$ is m. Next, form H' from H by deleting two elements of H and taking the median of $H' \cup L \cup \{x_{k+2}\}$. If the value is m, then $x_{k+2} < m$. If the value is greater than m, then

$x_{k+2} > m$. The value cannot be less than m. Having ranked x_{k+2} with respect to m, we can now form L' by deleting an element of L and finding the medians of length k in

$$H \cup \{x_{k+2}\} \cup L' - \{x_i\}$$

for each $x_i \in H \cup \{x_{k+2}\}$. One value will occur as the answer all but one time. This value is the value of the element missing from that query.

Reducing the complexity of this algorithm to $O(\log^2 k)$ involves a more careful construction of the sets H and L, forming a balanced set and ranking of another element as above.

Finally, we consider the case where nonuniqueness is not assumed and the overlap among queries is limited. In this case, we define $M(n,k,r)$ to be the minimum number of k-median queries necessary to compromise a database of n elements with overlap between queries limited to r. In this case, we have:

$$M(n,k,1) \geq 3/4(k+1), \text{ for } k \geq 3,$$

and

$$M(m,k,1) \leq 3k-5, \text{ for } n \geq k^2 -2k+4.$$

The proof of the lower bound is similar to those given previously. We argue that at least $(k+1)/2$ of the elements involved in any query set must occur in a second query or their values are never needed. The overlap restriction says that at least (k+1)/2 new queries are needed to cover elements introduced in the first query. These queries are again limited in overlap and the ith such query may contain no more than i-1 elements from previous queries. So, the new queries must introduce a total of

$$\sum_{i=1}^{(k-1)/2} i = (k^2 - 1)/8$$

new elements which need to appear in other queries. And the overlap restriction limits the number of such elements to be added to a new query to (k-1)/2, requiring (k+1)/4 new queries. Thus we have a total of

$$1+(k-1)/2 + (k+1)/4 = 3/4(k+1)$$

queries.

The upper bound involves manipulating the overlap restriction. We generalize the argument which gave the upper bound of 3 above in the unlimited general case. We assume the database elements are addressed as x_0, x_{ij}, for $1 \leq i,j \leq t$, and y_1 and y_2, where t=k-1 and q=k-2. The queries are then

$$Q_i = \mathrm{MEDIAN}\{x_0, x_{i1} \ldots, x_{it}\} \;,\; 1 \leq i \leq t$$

$$R_i = \mathrm{MEDIAN}\{y_1, x_{1i}, \ldots, x_{ti}\} \;,\; 1 \leq i \leq q$$

$$S_i = \mathrm{MEDIAN}\{y_2, x_{1,i+1}, x_{2,i+2}, \ldots, x_{ti}\},\; 1 \leq i \leq q,$$

with results to all Q queries being a, results to all R queries being b and results to all S queries being c, where $c<a<b$. It is easy to show now that $x_0=a$ by showing that $x_0 \leq 0$ and $x_0 \geq 0$.

3.3.4. Lying Data Bases. Median queries lead to another generalization. Suppose that a database consists of n elements and that all queries are of size k, with overlap restricted to 1. Suppose further that all queries are submitted to an "oracle" who answers by choosing any element of the query set for a response. Furthermore, this oracle can answer in any manner whatsoever to protect the database. We may even assume that the oracle receives all queries before answering a single query. Although such an oracle intuitively has a great advantage in keeping the database secure, we will see that compromise is not very difficult. In fact, if R(n,k) is the complexity of compromise for this model, then:

$$R(n,k) \leq 4k^2.$$

Compromise involves essentially constructing a finite projective plane. That is, all we need to show is the existence of $M = m(k)$ sets Q_i, for $1 \leq i \leq M$, such that $|Q_i \cap Q_j| \leq 1$ and each is a query on the elements $\{x_i | i \leq M-1\}$. Clearly, then the uniqueness of the elements guarantees compromise by the pigeon-hole principle. If k is a prime power, there is a projective plane of order k which is a system of k^2+k+1 sets chosen from k+1 of the k^2+k+1 database elements, each pair of sets having exactly one element in common. Deleting one query from the system and removing all of its elements leaves k^2+k queries of size k on a database of k^2. If k is not a power of a prime, there is surely a prime p, $k \leq p \leq 2k$, so that the construction for this prime p can be reduced to a construction for the desired k, while only adding a factor of 4 to the complexity of the entire construction.

3.3.5. Combinatorial Inference. The database problem is a special instance of a more basic type of problem: Given a finite set X, to infer properties of elements of X on the basis of "queries" regarding subsets of X. Besides the database security problem, the following combinatorial problems can also be formulated in this way.

<u>Function Identification</u>: determine the structure of a computer program by observing selected parameters of its operation.

<u>Group Testing</u>: a group of blood samples is to be processed rapidly to identify diseased persons. This is accomplished by mixing samples to determine whether or not any members of a set of subjects is infected and identified for further samples. The disease is such that sets of carriers of different strains can negate each others' effects in certain situations.

<u>Balance Problems</u>: given a number of objects of some standard weight β and two defective objects which weigh slightly more and less than β but are otherwise undistinguished, isolate the defective objects by weighings on a k-arm balance.

<u>Multidimensional Search</u>: given an algebraically defined set X, does X determine a point y (for example X may be a set of linear varieties, one of which may contain y).

<u>Coin Weighing</u>: by choosing X from {1,...,k} and allowing queries of the form "what is $|S_i \cap X|$?", $S_i \subseteq \{1,\ldots,k\}$, to determine X.

All of the aspects of database problems are interesting in this more general setting. We may vary the choice of primitives by allowing suitably restricted queries. The problem may be to insure that k queries always solve the problem or to determine minimal values of k needed to solve the problem. General audit problems (proving upper and lower bounds on the complexity of determining whether or not a given sequence of queries allows the appropriate inference) and enumeration problems (determine the number of "unsafe problems" for a given number of queries) are also important.

3.4 Bibliographic Notes. The first published work on protection models is [37]. Their research was heavily influenced by the PhD Dissertation of Jones [44]. A number of diverse and interesting models appears in the work of Jones, Lipton and Snyder [4, 8, 9, 54, 84]. Much of section 3.3 is drawn from [25].

Parker's case studies gives a good overview of the security threats modern computers face [64]. Other surveys that are helpful are [24,15,72]. The papers of [19] also lend a current perspective.

The Bell and LaPadula model is presented in [2], while the application of this model to kernelized systems is presented in [62]. The proceedings of the 1979 summer school on security [26] describe the current state of technology for the various kernel projects. The specification [33] is a complete specification of KSOS-11. A critical evaluation of verification technology is offered in [18].

The concept of confinement is defined in [50], where the examples of leakage channels are also to be found.

Other inference mechanisms which illustrate the ease with which information may be extracted from software systems have been proposed in the context of database systems [14,16,17,29,69].

4. Protocols and Security

One of the main themes of the software oriented security models is the uncontrollability of software properties. The sheer size of a computer operating system prohibits its complete and detailed examination. Even correctness proofs that seek to establish security properties of such systems leave large portions of the systems unexamined and usually explicitly assume that some of the software is to be 'trusted'. When the software can be treated formally, the fact that the software mediates the system security <u>and</u> delivers services to the user makes the security of the system suspect: it is very difficult to insure that the inherent functionality of the system cannot be exploited to compromise the system

There are other weaknesses in the software-oriented approaches to security. For example, software information channels are 'hidden'; that is to say, they are conceptual and logical paths for information that can be observed only in the sense that one can in principle duplicate program execution, but they cannot be rigorously monitored. In particular, system compromise may go completely undetected by the software, and there does not appear to be any way to insure that system compromises are associated with observable events. Another weakness of the software approach to security lies in its attempt to isolate users without recourse to the notion of 'secrecy.'

A way around these difficulties lies in utilizing security protocols based on cryptography.

We will assume a model of computation which generalizes the cryptographic channel defined in Chapter 2. That is, we assume a system of relatively secure, autonomous processing and storage resources interconnected by communications media, or _channels_. As usual, the channels are assumed to be insecure and subject to attack. The normal activities of the system consist of periods during which the resources carry out actions which are generally not visible to an observer of the channel. These periods are interspersed with _transactions_ - logical units of communication activity.

A _protocol_ is an algorithm for implementing a class of transactions. Protocols for even moderately sophisticated transactions involve a complex layering of processes and capabilities. At the lowest level there is a single message over the channel. The principle technique for implementing such a capability is the _cryptographic_ concealment of the message. Until quite recently, research efforts on secure protocols have concentrated on the security of the underlying cryptographic transformations. But new protocols have arisen whose security properties are not readily apparent. In these protocols, it is not only the security of the cryptosystem that plays a role; even _assuming as an axiom_ the perfect concealment of messages, the _logic_ of the protocols or even the implementation of the cryptosystem may be flawed. Such flaws, when undetected, are as damaging to overall security as a compromised cryptosystem.

Protocols have a number of pragmatic advantages. First, protocols can be separated from the software which delivers services to the user. Second, protocols are generally high level constructions which can be examined in detail. Third, protocols can be implemented using hardware or hardware-isolated software so that all communication channels are explicit and observable. This in effect rules out covert software channels.

As a simple example of how cryptographic protocols can be used to insure that systems meet all sorts of security properties (in particular, properties besides secrecy), let us return briefly to the Lucifer sytem. Recall that the Lucifer system is a S/P network-based cryptosystem -- a direct predecessor of DES -- whose main purpose is to provide authentication security. Recall also that one of the cryptographic advantages of Lucifer is the 'strong interdependence among digits' which guarantees that message corruption is easily detectable. Thus the messages of the system are, in a sense, tamper-proof.

To use Lucifer as an authentication scheme a device called a <u>password generator</u> is required. Although the device is transparent to the transmitter, its purpose is to seed the transmitted message with a secret stamp, whose corruption signals the receiver that an enemy has attempted to manipulate the message (or that the message has been accidentally corrupted by noise on the channel). The process of encipherment keeps an enemy from knowing just where in the cipher to look for message bits and password bits. The receiver upon decipherment of the transmission should be able to read a clean copy of the password, and his action in accepting or rejecting the transmission is dependent upon being able to do so. Figure 4.1 depicts the Lucifer Password scheme.

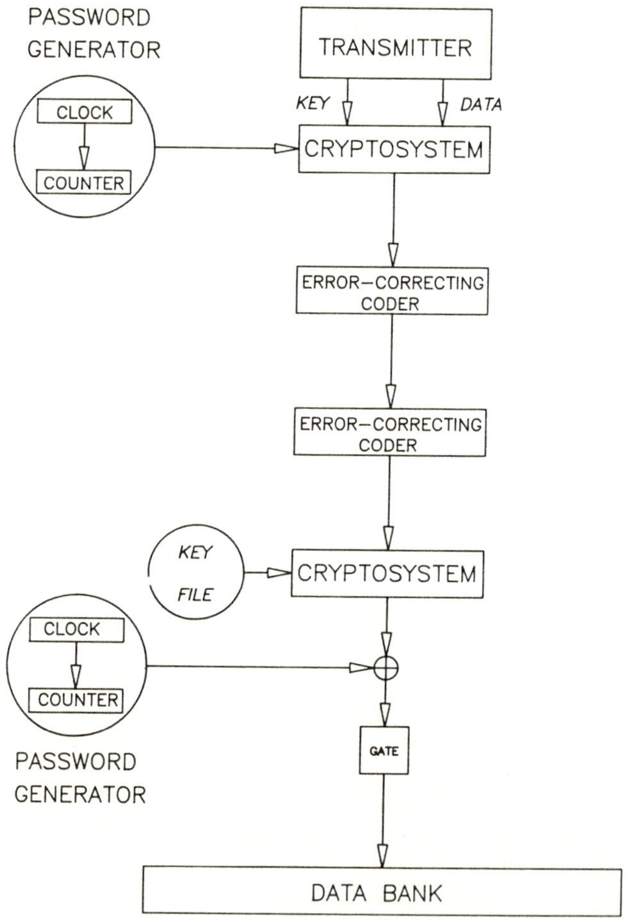

Figure 4.1
The LUCIFER Authentication Protocol

The protocol behaves in the following way. A subscriber to the system is issued a card that has encoded on a magnetic strip his cryptographic key. The receiver has recorded the key for each user in a secret file that will be used to drive the decrypting operation. By inserting the card into an appropriate device and entering data, the transmitter is able to send blocks of 64 bit messages to the receiver. The transmission is preceded by a sequence of messages which identify the user to the receiver and allow the retrieval of the appropriate key from the key file.

Each 64 bit block is submitted to the enciphering device along with a 'time stamp' generated by a scheme as shown above. A clock and a binary counter provides a unique sequence of stamps. From now on we will refer to any such scheme as a <u>time stamp</u> scheme.

It is essential in the Lucifer system only that the time stamps constitute a reproducible nonrepeating sequence and we shall take this to be the defining characteristic of all time stamp generators.

The S/P network enciphers the message-time stamp, encodes it for noisy channel transmission and sends the message to the receiver. The receiver, who has already retrieved the key for the user transmitting the message, now decrypts the transmission, block by block, and -- having a local capability of reproducing the transmitter's time stamp sequence -- attempts to match the time stamp of the message received with the local time stamp. If the receiver should ever fail to match, he sounds an alarm and announces that an attempt has been made to send a corrupted message. If the channel is noisy, the error correcting coder recovers the lost bits and restores the original message. But noisy channel codes work only for white noise. If the errors are not sporadic, the interdependence property of Lucifer causes a garbled deciphered text and the time stamp will not be recoverable. As for authentication, clearly, an enemy cannot intercept a transmission and store it, hoping to retransmit it on his own.

4.1 Arbiters. _Arbiters_ are important tools in designing secure protocols. An arbiter is a trusted system component that acts as an intermediary between mutually suspicious users. Oftentimes, the only apparent way to devise a protocol meeting certain requirements is to invoke an arbiter. Consider, for example, the problem of exchanging hostages. A and B each hold messages as "hostages". That is, A holds a message that B wants to receive and B holds a message equally valuable to A; (e.g., a secret that is to be exchanged or a signed check). In the presence of an arbiter, exchanging hostages becomes a simple matter. A, B and the arbiter enter into a mutual agreement to transfer their hostages through the arbiter. The arbiter then waits a specified length of time for the hostages, checks the authenticity of the hostages, and sends them to the appropriate destination. If the transaction is not completed for some reason, the arbiter must return the messages it has received to the originator.

The arbiter is usually not directly required in the actual

transaction implemented by the protocol; the extra communication, which may be costly, is solely for security purposes. The establishment and maintenance of an arbiter trusted by each participant is itself likely to be costly, if indeed it is possible. Arbiters in high demand may also create bottlenecks in a system. These considerations often justify a search for secure, non-arbitrated protocols, even in cases in which simple arbitrated solutions exist.

Because of the cost of arbitration, some arbitrated protocols are actually logically composed of two lower-level protocols. One is a frequently executed, non-arbitrated protocol, and the other is an arbitrated protocol executed under exceptional conditions. Signed contracts are examples of such _adjudicable_ protocols; the potential for verification in court (the arbitrated sub-protocol) is sufficient to guarantee compliance with a contract under most conditions. Indeed, the arbiter in most adjudicable protocols is a human judge! _'Adjudicator'_ will be used to distinguish this special type of arbiter, while 'arbiter' will generally denote third parties active during all or most executions of a protocol.

4.2. Digital Signatures. The time stamp scheme described above is, in a sense, a way of _signing_ messages. More generally, a _digital signature_ scheme is a protocol which cryptographically attaches an identifying mark (the 'signature') to a message in such a way that the transmitter cannot later disavow the mark as his own. Of course, receivers should be unable to forge signatures, but unlike traditional -- i.e., paper and pen -- signatures a digital signature should be bound to the message so that once the authenticity of the signature is established, the authenticity of the document should also be established. It should, for example, be impossible to alter the signed message after the signature is affixed. A unique feature of the concept of a signature is its relation to legal status. In using signed documents of any kind, disputes arise that are submitted to an authority for adjudication. A signature protocol should allow an adjudicator of a dispute to settle the dispute in favor of the correct party with arbitrarily small chance of error.

Therefore, a digital signature protocol should allow users to satisfy the following properties in such a way that any disputes can be decided with arbitrarily small probability of error on the part of the judge.

1. If S(P,M) is the signature by person P on the message M, then it should be impossible for any one other than P to produce any pairs (M,S(P,M)).
2. If a purported message-signature pair (M,W) is received, and if it is claimed that W represents P's signature on M, then the receiver must be able to check W=S(P,M).

Notice that in property (1), it is not possible for any one other than P to produce a message signed by P. If someone other than P could produce even one message N≠M such that S(P,M) = S(P,N), then that person could offer N as a message signed by P, contradicting the immutability of a signed message.

4.2.1. Conventional Approaches. The signature protocols based on traditional cryptosystems like DES and Lucifer assume that the signatures are to be arbitrated by a trusted third party at the time the message is transmitted. Figure 4.2 illustrates the organization of an arbitrated system.

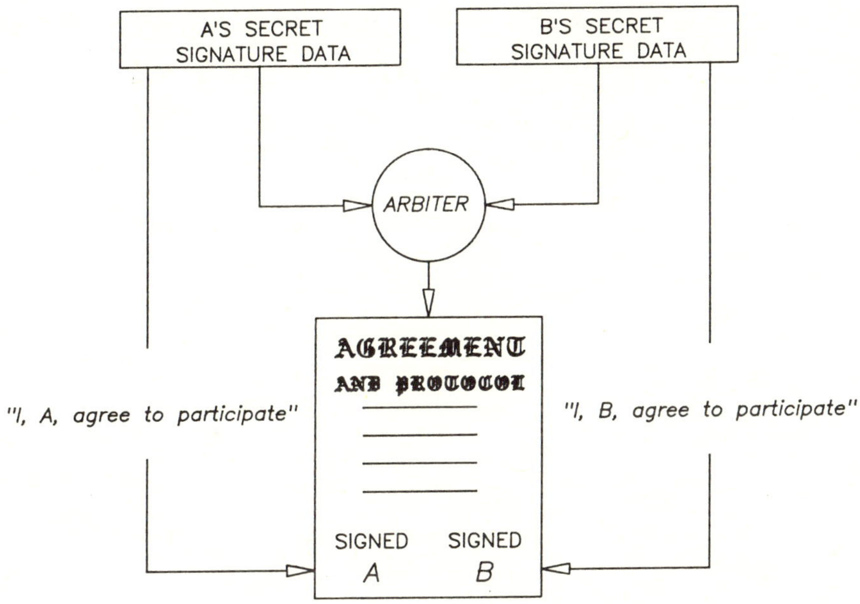

Figure 4.2
Arbitrated Signature Protocol

Obviously, the arbiter has access to a great deal of secret information. Therefore, great care must be taken to insure the trustworthiness of the arbiter. In implementations, arbiters are sometimes combinations of hardware and software systems which reside at a special site in a communications network.

The security property being exploited in arbitrated schemes is message authentication. The recipient of a signed message in such a scheme can convince himself of the security of the transmission, but he may not be able to convince an adjudicator -- this is a fatal weakness of simple arbitrated protocols.

We will assume that the participants have a cryptosystem like the DES available and that each (We will name them A,B,C,...) has his own key K_A, K_B, ... In addition to keeping his own key secret, each user shares his key with the arbiter. The arbiter will be able to authenticate messages from each user since he (the arbiter) knows each user's key. Likewise, users can authenticate messages from the arbiter.

We will assume that the message to be signed is composed of n blocks $X_1,\ldots,X_n$. Block X_{n+1} is added to the message and consists of an arbitrary plaintext pattern whose composition has been agreed upon by both the sending and receiving parties. This protocol makes essential use of a 'noise vector' V which is a 64 bit random vector that is used to scramble transmissions; however, for many applications, the time stamping scheme described for the Lucifer systems is entirely adequate to insure that the transmission is secure.

To initiate the protocol, user A uses chained feedback block encryption to form ciphertext $C=C_1,\ldots,C_n$ and signature $S(K_A,X_1\ldots X_n) = C_{n+1}$ by the following equations:

$$C_1 = E(K_A, X_1 \oplus V)$$
$$C_2 = E(K_A, X_2 \oplus C1 \oplus X_1)$$
$$\ldots$$
$$C_{n+1} = E(K_A, X_{n+1} \oplus C_n \oplus X_n).$$

The message $(V, C, S(K_A, X_1 \ldots X_n))$ is sent to the arbiter. Deciphering the message is carried out in symmetrical fashion:

$$X_1 = D(K_A, C_1) \oplus V$$
$$X_2 = D(K_A, C_2) \oplus C_1 \oplus X_1$$
$$\ldots$$
$$X_{n+1} = D(K_A, C_{n+1}) \oplus C_n \oplus X_n.$$

The arbiter then checks the value of X_{n+1}. Because the deciphered value of X_{n+1} is a complicated function of K_A, V and C, the decipherment of the signature with the wrong key or a change in one or more bits of C will cause the value of X_{n+1} to be incorrect. If the arbiter sees that X_{n+1} is the correct value, he concludes that $(C, S(K_A, X_1 \ldots X_n))$ was sent by A and that $X_1 \ldots X_n$ is the true content of the message sent by A. If the arbiter cannot verify this, he concludes that the message is not genuine. The arbiter in either circumstance generates a message M which is sent to the recipient B:

$$M = (X_1 \ldots, X_n, V, S(K_A, X_1 \ldots X_n), \text{ ALARM}),$$

where the value of ALARM is defined as follows:

$$\text{ALARM} = \begin{cases} 0, & \text{if message was genuine} \\ 1, & \text{otherwise.} \end{cases}$$

This message is enciphered using K_B and is sent to B just as the original message was sent to the arbiter. Receiver B then accepts the original message if the version of M that it receives is genuine, the ALARM setting for a genuine M is 'off', and M satisfies any ancillary agreements (e.g, message formats, passwords) that have been entered into by A and B.

In case of subsequent disputes, it may be helpful to archive certain of these transmissions. For example, B should probably retain $(V, X_1 \ldots, X_n, C_{n+1})$ in order to be able to prove receipt of plaintext. The protocol is executed anew to effect such a proof.

Aside from the adjudication problems of this protocol, the signature $S(K_A, \ldots)$ does satisfy the properties of a digital signature.

Notice that errors in transmission can be filtered out of the scheme by the same techniques used in the Lucifer system.

4.2.2. Lamport's Algorithm. This protocol is based on a traditional cipher like the DES. Suppose that an n bit message M is to be signed. The transmitter of the message randomly generates 2r cryptographic keys,

$$k_1, K_1, \ldots, k_r, K_r,$$

which are kept in secret. As part of their agreement to communicate, the transmitter gives to the receiver 2r blocks of validation parameters:

$$u_1, U_1, \ldots, u_r, U_r$$

as well as their corresponding ciphertext under DES,

$$E(k_1,u_1), E(K_1,U_1), \ldots, E(k_r,u_r), E(K_r,U_r).$$

It is probably desirable that these parameters be registered with a trusted authority, since the receiver will need to insure the validity of the transmission by comparing received parameters with the agreed-upon parameters.

The signature consists of 56n bits for n bit M generated from the message and the keys k_i, K_i as follows. If the ith bit of the message is 0, then the ith 56 bit block of the signature is k_i, otherwise the ith block of the signature is K_i.

When the receiver sees the message and signature, he validates the signature by reading the ith bit of the message, for all $i=1,\ldots,n$. If the ith bit is 0 and the ith 56 bit block of the signature is S_i, he checks $E(S_i,u_i) = E(k_i,u_i)$. If the ith bit is 1, he checks to see if S_i will encipher U_i correctly.

By using a <u>compressed encoding</u>, it is possible to reduce the size of the signature considerably. If the message is divided into 56 bit blocks $X_1,\ldots,X_n$, they can be treated as DES keys and a compressed encoding of the message M can be obtained by

$$CE(M) = E(X_n, E(\ldots, E(X_2, E(X_1, c))\ldots)),$$

where c is a fixed constant called the 'standard message'. Then the number of 56 bit keys that make up the signature is determined by the length of CE(M) rather than the length of M by selecting according to the parity of the bits of CE(M) as before: since the compressed encoding of c is 64 bits in length, the total signature size is of constant length 3,584 bits. Since there are 2^n messages and $2^{(n-64)}$ with the same CE, it should be computationally hard to search an $M' \neq M$ with the same compressed encoding.

4.2.3 Rabin's Algorithm. Rabin's scheme tackles the adjudication issue. As in the protocol above, the tansmitter generates secret keys, again 2r of them: $k_1, k_2, \ldots, k_{2r}$. Validaton parameters $u_1, u_2, \ldots$ and their ciphers $E(k_1, u_1), E(k_2, u_2)$ are exchanged and registered for later use. To sign M, the transmitter works with $M' = CE(M)$; specifically, he enciphers M' with each of his 2r keys:

$$E(k_1, M'), \ldots, E(k_{2r}, M').$$

The receiver can validate the message-signature pair by asking the transmitter to send him at random r of the keys used in the transmission. To insure that the transmitter selects the keys at random, the receiver may specify the indices of the keys he wants received; We will describe in a moment the mechanism whereby it is guaranteed that the transmitter must send the keys asked for. Once the receiver has the keys from the transmitter, he checks them using the public validation parameters and their ciphers (e.g., if the key k is one of those requested by the receiver, then if k is alleged to be k_i, the receiver checks $E(k, u_i) = E(k_i, u_i)$.

If the transmitter disputes that the message was signed by him, he produces for the judge all of his keys $k_1, \ldots k_{2r}$. These keys and the signature are validated using the validation parameters as before. If r+1 or more of the signature elements are correct, then the receiver is judged to have a message signed by the transmitter, and the transmitter is judged to be trying to disavow a message that he has signed. If r or fewer of the elements in the signature are correct, then it is judged that the receiver is attempting to forge the message or signature.

What is the probability of fooling the adjudicator? Suppose that the transmitter has been able to successfully disavow his message. Then r or fewer of the signature elements are correct. But since the receiver validated the signature, there must be exactly r correct entries and furthermore, the receiver must have randomly selected exactly these r. The probability of such an event is $1/\binom{2r}{r}$

4.2.4. Public Key Signatures. The defining properties of public key systems make them automatically suited to signature protocols. To sign M, A makes use of his public key P_A and his secret key S_A. A first forms $D(S_A,M) = C$ and sends it to B. Since B knows A's public key, B can recover M by

$$E(P_A,C) = E(P_A,D(S_A,M)) = M.$$

Since M has now been revealed to B, B can use the contents of M to validate the message, and C is the proof that M originated with A. By the secrecy of S_A and the complexity of inverting the public key functions, only A could have produced $D(S_A,M) = C$.

The message cannot be changed since public key systems are necessarily good random number generators. Suppose that the message length is m. If C is enciphered with any key other than P_A or if a corrupted value of C is enciphered, the probability of producing a correct value for M is about 2^{-m}.

There are knapsack problems which are useful for signature schemes. A <u>signature</u> <u>knapsack</u> is based on the following problem: given n, S, a, find a vector x (each $0 \leq x_i \leq \log n$) such that S = $a \cdot x \bmod n$.

As usual, a <u>message</u> is interpreted as a vector x so that encryption with public key k = (a,n) is given by

$$E_k(x) = x \cdot a = S'.$$

Thus, given $S = E_k(x)$, recovering x requires solving the knapsack which is NP-complete. Suppose that the owner of the public key K = (a,n) = $((a_1,\ldots,a_{2k}),n)$ determines a by choosing secretly and at random 2k² values h_{ij} ($1 \leq i \leq k_1$, $1 \leq j \leq 2k$) and letting $a_1,\ldots,a_{2k}$ be any values satisfying the k equations.

$$\sum_{j=1}^{2k} h_{ij} a_j = 2^{i-1} \bmod n.$$

To sign a message S, form

$$D_{K'}(S) = (S)^R \cdot (h_{ij}),$$

where $(S)^R$ is the vector of bits formed by writing in reverse order the binary representations of S, and $(h_{ij}) = K'$ is the secret key used for signatures. To check a signature x of a message S, a recipient computes

$$E_K(x) = E_K(D_{K'}(S)).$$

If $(S)^R = (s_1,\ldots,s_k)$, then

$$E_K(x) = x \cdot a \bmod n$$

$$= (S^R) \cdot (h_{ij}) \cdot \underline{a} \bmod n$$

$$= \sum_{j=1}^{2k} \left(\sum_{i=1}^{k} s_i \, h_{ij} \right) a_j \bmod n$$

$$= \sum_{i=1}^{k} s_i \, 2^{i-1} \bmod n = S.$$

In addition to the RSA 1-1 public key function, for which the protocol above is directly applicable, there are public key functions which purport to offer enhanced security. One such function is the 4-1 function

$$E_{(n,b)}(M) = M(M+b) \bmod n,$$

whose properties were examined in Section 2.4.3. To sign a message M using this function, a random vector V is appended to the message M:

$$M' = (M,V).$$

To sign M, the transmitter forms CE(M'), and checks the solubility of

$$x(x+b) = CE(M') \bmod n,$$

which can be done quickly by anyone knowing n=pq. If the equation is not soluble, then a new random V is generated. The expected number of trials before a soluble congruence is generated is constant (≤ 4). The signature is then (V,x).

4.2.5. Authentication. Based on the idea of signing messages using the fact that D and E are inverses, a number of protocols can be constructed that differ in their methods of resolving disputes. Some of these methods have already been discussed above for conventional ciphers. For example, in the simple public key protocol, A has no recourse if his private key is compromised in some fashion -- in that case anyone can duplicate A's signature.

By using time stamps, a protocol can be established that gives A protection in case his key is compromised. The time stamp protocol uses an arbiter to mediate the claims of key lossage and to keep current records concerning the status of keys. When asked, the arbiter will sign documents that indicate that a secret key has not been reported lost as of the current time. These documents are called <u>validity checks</u>.

To communicate, A sends $D(S_A,M)$ to B, which B immediately has time stamped. B then obtains a validity check from the arbiter, and, if A has already reported his key as lost, B should certainly reject C as having not originated with A. An adjudicator would then find that A had sent the message if it encrypted properly and if it had been time stamped before any loss of key was reported to the arbiter.

Witnessing signatures becomes very easy in public key systems. For example, a witness, C -- agrees upon in advance by A and by B -- forms

$$D(S_C, \text{'I saw A sign M'}).$$

4.3. Mental Poker. A common problem in systems that exchange messages concerns the verification of the messages -- in particular, the fairness of message exchanges.

The 'mental poker' problem is an abstraction of just such problems. The game of mental poker has rules just like the ordinary game of poker, except that no cards are actually exchanged and that everyone in the game is a potential cheater. The properties of the deal that must be preserved in a solution to the mental poker problem are that each player must know the cards that are in his hand but have no information about the cards that are in the other players' hands. The dealer should distribute all possible hands with equal probability and should not allow the same card to appear in two hands simultaneously. In playing the game, a player should be able to discard from his own hand and reveal cards from his own hand without compromising the rest of his hand. Finally, any participant must be able to verify that the preceding game has been fairly played. According to the Shannon theory of cryptanalysis, such a game is theoretically impossible. Suppose that A and B play a one card (each) game with the deck $\{c_1, c_2, c_3\}$. All that A and B can do is exchange messages, and after the message exchanges they must know not only their own hands, but also that the game has been fairly played. Suppose that after exchanging the sequence of messages M, A receives card c_i and B receives c_j, where $j \neq i$. Obviously, M cannot reveal one player's hand to the other player. Let $S_M(A)$ be the set of cards which A can possibly hold after the exhange M, and let $S_M(B)$ be defined similarly. $|S_M|$ is the analog of the random variable N(m) in the unconditional theory. We claim $|S_M(A)|=|S_M(B)|=2$, which leads immediately to the contradiction that there is a legal deal in which A and B can hold the same card. If $S_M(A)=1$, then there is no uncertainty about A's hand, so B will guess the proper card. On the other hand, if $S_M(A)=3$, then $S_M(B)=\emptyset$, which is not a legal deal. Thus, $S_M(A)=2$. The argument for B is identical.

However, there is a public key protocol that does allow the game to be played as described above.

The idea behind the protocol is to imagine that there are cards to be distributed and that they have each been placed in a box that can be locked with a padlock. Player B locks each box with a padlock to which he has the key, and player A selects five boxes to return to B for his hand (A cannot have seen these since they were locked by B). A selects his own hand and places his own lock on these five boxes next to B's lock. Notice again that A cannot have peeked at his own hand due to B's lock. A then returns the double-locked boxes to B. B has now in his possession the ten locked boxes from which he removes all of these locks. Since five boxes are still locked, he then returns the boxes with A's lock remaining to player A. A removes his lock and the game can continue. By revealing the keys used at the end of the game, both players can determine that the cards claimed to be dealt were in fact dealt.

In the protocol, locking the box with a card in it, is equivalent to encrypting a message 'ace of clubs', 'deuce of hearts', etc. with a secret key. Let n be a large odd number with a factorization that is known to A and B. The encryption function used by A and B with encryption key K is

$$E(K,M) = M^K \pmod{n},$$

where,

$$(K, \phi(n)) = 1.$$

Correspondingly, the decryption function is

$$D(K,C) = C^{L} (\text{mod } n),$$

where,

$$LK = 1 (\text{mod } \phi(n)).$$

E and D satisfy all of the properties of complexity based ciphers and the important additional property that the encryptions commute:

$$\begin{aligned} E(K,E(J,M)) &= M^{JK} (\text{mod } n) \\ &= M^{KJ} (\text{mod } n) \\ &= E(J,E(K,M)). \end{aligned}$$

So that the 'padlocks' can be assumed to be commutative as is required by the protocol.

A sends each message encrypted with his secret key to B. A then randomly selects five ciphertext messages $C_1,..C_5$ and sends them to B. A randomly selects five more messages $C_6,...C_{10}$ and forms $D_i=E(A,C_i)$, where $6 \leq i \leq 10$ and 'A' denotes A's secret key. The messages $D_6,..D_{10}$ are then sent to B. B forms the messages $C'_i=D(B,D_i)$ and sends the C' messages to A who decrypts: $M_i = D(A,C'_i)$. By the commutativity of the operations, this recovers the proper hand for A. The safety of the protocol is apparent from the lock-box analogy.

The generalization to several players follows in much the same fashion. We will not describe the protocol for resolving disputes, even though --- as we pointed out for digital signatures -- this may be the factor which determines the suitability of a protocol for practical use.

4.4 Secret Ballot Elections. If an election were held over a computer network, how could the voters insure that it was a fair election, that only registered voters voted, and that no one could properly associate any voter with his vote, except his own? The protocol described below provides exactly this utility. We describe a three-voter election.

The election protocol employs three encryption functions -- public-key encryption, public-key signatures, and a third function in which a random string is concatenated to the message before coding with the receiver's public key so that a matching of plaintext-ciphertext pairs is possible only for the sender and receiver, provided neither divulges the random string. None of these functions is commutative, and the signature is not the inverse of either encryption function. Before execution of the protocol begins, each user has a correct, ordered voter registration list, including each voter's public key. The encryption, signature and randomization functions are E, S, and R, respectively. Each voter has a unique vote v_{name}. Thus, A has signature function S_A and vote v_A. In a real election, in which the set of possible votes is small, votes could be created by concatenating a fixed number of random bits to the real vote. Each voter encrypts his vote as

$R_A R_B R_C E_A E_B E_C(v_{name})$.

All of these messages are sent to one voter, say A, who decrypts the first randomization and forwards them, in random order, to B. B checks that his own vote, in the proper stage of decryption, is in the set he receives. If so, he decrypts the next layer and forwards the votes in random order -- if not, he stops executing the protocol. After C decrypts the last level of randomization, the votes are sent again to every voter in succession. This time, provided a voter's vote is again properly included in the set, he signs the votes and broadcasts the signatures to all voters. He also removes the next level of encryption, and forwards the votes to the next voter. Finally, C broadcasts the decrypted votes. Each voter accepts the election results if the signatures he receives actually match the properly encrypted votes, and if his own vote is in the set.

4.5 Password Authentication. Password protection schemes in computer systems have long used a primitive cryptographic protocols to insure the integrity of the password file and to authenticate passwords as they are submitted by users (cf. the Lucifer system discussed above). Let f(x) be a cryptographically secure transformation (or _1-way function_); i.e., a function of x that is easy to compute but difficult to invert. In the simple scheme, f(x) is stored in the computer in place of the password x, avoiding possible compromise of the password by a system intruder. In the absence of encryption, it is still possible for an attacker to record x during transmission and use this knowledge to masquerade as the user at a later time.

Suppose now that the scheme stores $f^{1000}(x)$ in the computer instead of f(x). The correct password for the i'th terminal session is $f^{1000-i}(x)$. Upon receiving a value y as a password for the i'th user login, the central site authenticates y by computing $f^{i}(y)$ and comparing with the stored value $f^{1000}(x)$. Passwords must, of course, be reinitialized every thousand logins.

Simple extensions to this basic scheme permit secure resynchronization between the central site and the users. Backing up the system without reusing old passwords is also possible.

Note that this protocol does not prevent an attacker from compromising a communications link and masquerading as a system user after the password authentication has been completed. Additional protection must be provided to extend authentication throughout the terminal session.

4.6 Using Randomness. Random choice is a powerful tool in the design of secure protocols. It is the very basis of the information theoretic approach to cryptography. The power of randomization stems from two principles. First, if one or more participants in a protocol is forced to make a random choice in order to successfully complete the protocol, then the fact that the resulting sets of actions are no longer determined can be used to smooth out any "first-move" advantages. Second, randomness can be used to approximate the ideal security conditions of the Shannon models.

The basic building block for several protocols which exploit randomness is the oblivious transfer. The important property of the oblivious transfer which makes it useful for secure protocol design is that it insures a certain fairness in transactions. The idea is that A can send a message to B but not be certain about which message was actually received.

Suppose A and B wish to toss a fair coin over the telephone. Just as in the poker example, neither is willing to trust the other. A begins by selecting two large prime numbers p and q, and sends the product N = pq to B. The factors of N are secret. B is judged to have won the coin toss if he can factor N. B now selcts (randomly) a number x in the interval 1 to N and computes x^2mod N = y, which he sends back to A. A extracts the four square roots of y mod N. A does not at this point know which of the four roots have absolute value x. With probability 0.5 of choosing x or -x, A sends one of the roots to B. If B receives x, he does not have enough information to factor N, but if B receives one of the other roots of y, say z, he can form x+z. The greatest common divisor of x+z and N is a factor of N, so B can factor N by the Euclidean algorithm.

Notice that A must send a number N which can be factored. If N is itself a prime number (or a power of a prime), then B always loses. This problem can be dealt with by allowing B to test to see if N is a prime number. Ordinarily, this would be as difficult as factoring N, but by using a probabilistic test for primality, B can, very quickly, and with small probability of error determine whether or not N is prime. Furthermore, A does not know if he has allowed B to factor N or not.

The fact that A does not know if B actually has enough information to factor, results in a <u>weak</u> <u>coin-toss</u>: B can always choose to lose the toss, but in order to win, he must be able to produce the factors of N.

The oblivious transfer can be applied to the problem of sending <u>certified</u> <u>mail</u>. In sending certified mail, the sender is to be given a receipt that the mail was received. Unlike regular certified mail, however, this protocol also insures that the contents of the received mail is what was sent.

As in coin flipping, the idea is to transfer factors of large numbers obliviously. A generates ten large public keys (products of large primes) and successively encrypts the message to be sent with these keys. To recover the message, B must obtain all decrypting keys by factoring the ten encrypting keys. In the first stage of the algorithm B and A run oblivious transfers for all ten keys. After the first stage is complete, B will most likely not be able to factor all ten keys, so the algorithm proceeds to second and third stages until B has enough information to recover all the keys. The expected number of stages for B is quite small (four in this case).

The messages A receives from B constitute a receipt and during adjudication of a dispute, A could convince a judge that B had been sent enough information to factor all ten keys.

Other applications of the oblivious transfer include protocols for exchanging secrets, playing mental poker and signing contracts.

4.7 Key Distribution. Ease of key distribution in a cryptosystem is a factor in judging the security of the system. For example, in arbitrated signature systems, a central repository of keys is necessary and the safety of the protocol is limited by the safety of this repository. we have, in fact, described a special protocol -- the time stamping protocol -- for dealing with the problem of key lossage.

A general question concerning key distribution is whether or not cryptographic techniques can be applied to yield distribution protocols. A simple protocol that assumes only standard cryptographic capabilities is the so-called _centralized key distribution protocol_. In this protocol, A and B each deposit conventional crytographic keys with a central key distribution center. Then for A to communicate with B, the center uses A's key and B's key to derive a key for the session which is distributed to both A and B. Although this protocol is widely used, it rests a great deal of responsibility with a central authority and ultimately reduces to the problem of distributing keys to the central authority.

Public key systems can be used to allow A and B to agree on a common key K without any prior secret agreements. To execute the protocol, A randomly selects an enciphering key K and a deciphering key K' and sends K to B. Then B picks at random a key k and transmits E(K,k) to A from which A recovers k by D(K',E(K,k)) = k. The key k can then be used for conventional cryptographic communication. Although the enemy cannot uncover k, he can interfere with the communication, and can even force a known value of k on A and B.

The standard public key communication protocols allow A and B to securely exchange session keys which can be combined to form a key k. This key is both secret and authenticated.

The major difficulty with this protocol is the alteration of public keys: this problem is avoided if they are certified by a central authority. This protocol ultimately reduces to the standard public key protocol in which A and B check each other's certificates in order to insure that each has the other's public key and not the key of an imposter. Aside from the trust placed in the central authority to issue good certificates, the strength of this system rests on the ability of the users to maintain the integrity of the central authority's private key.

One way to further authenticate entries in the file of public keys is to apply a one-way hash function to the entire file, resulting in a message of just a few hundred bits, called the root of the public file. By letting all valid users know the value of the root, then any user can authenticate the entire set of public keys by computing the hashing function of the file and comparing it to the root. Although this method of authentication eliminates use of secret keys for the central authority, it is obviously too inefficient. However, there are protocols based on this scheme that are both efficient and achieve the same effect.

4.8 Distributing Subkeys. A significant key distribution problem involves constructing keys from subkeys in such a way that loss of even a large fraction of the subkeys does not compromise the total key. Given a message M (e.g., a key) the problem is to divide M into pieces $M_1,\ldots,M_n$ in such a way that:

1. if k or more of the pieces is known then M is easily computable, and
2. knowledge of fewer than k pieces leaves M undetermined.

One protocol for solving this problem can be based on polynomial interpolation. M is divided into pieces by randomly choosing a k-1 degree polynomial q(x) with coefficients $a_0,\ldots,a_{k-1}$, where $a_0=M$. To form the 'pieces' M_i, one evaluates

$$M_1 = q(1),$$
$$M_2 = q(2)$$
$$\ldots$$
$$M_n = q(n).$$

Any k of these values determines the polynomial, but any number of values less than k does not determine q(x) and therefore M. By working in a finite field, polynomial evaluation and interpolation can be carried out by fast algorithms.

Even if defections are allowed, it is possible to reconstruct a master key in relatively efficient fashion. Suppose that the subkey problem also encompasses:

3. at most k-1 subkey defections are tolerable.

By a standard result of algebraic coding theory, a code of minimum distance d can correct $t < (d-1)/2$ errors, where a vector R is said to contain t errors if

$$R = E \oplus C,$$

for a vector with Hamming weight $W(E) = t$.

Let $W(E)=t$ and let E_0 be a random error vector $W(E_0)=t$ and E_1 be an error vector $W(E_1)=e$. Then to construct R (the master key) from the E_i's, it is only necessary to be able to correct t errors but not t+1,...:

$$W(\sum_{0<i\leq n} E_i) = t - e(n-k) > 0,$$

$$W(\sum_{0<i<k} E_{u_i}) = t + e,$$

and

$$W(\sum_{0<i\leq k} E_{u_i}) = t.$$

The index u_i represents the ith chosen user of a subkey, so that the fact that t errors are correctable but t+e are not correctable implies that conditions (2) and (3) are satisfied.

This protocol has the advantage of generalizing to <u>hierarchical</u> key distribution problems. Suppose that the subkey problem must be solved for an organization with L 'levels'; the level i has associated with it a key threshold k_i (i.e., k_i level i subkeys can construct a master key). The protocol above can be adapted by simply increasing key weights at level i:

$$W\left(\sum_{j=1}^{k_i} E_{u_j}\right) = t, \quad 1 \le u_j \le n$$

and

$$W\left(\sum_{j=1}^{k_i - 1} E_{u_j}\right) = t + e_i,$$

where e_i is the weight of the ith subkey. In this protocol, collusion is possible, but it requires a knowledge of the 'right' accomplices.

4.9 Shaking Hands. Handshaking protocols solve certain authentication problems common in communications environments. The problem is that A and B want to establish a secure communications channel without a prior exchange of cryptographic keys. A solution should allow A to generate a message M such that M is comprehensible only to B and when B receives the message, he should be convinced that M was sent by A. We will present two protocols; one based on a conventional cryptosystem, the other based on a public key system. Both protocols use a central authority to whom A has passed secret cryptographic information (i.e., a secret key) and a time stamp generator with all the properties described above. A* and B* are taken to be the secret names of A and B -- A is known to B as A* and B is known to A as A*. To shake hands with B, A first sends **request**$(A^*, B^*, E_A(t))$, where t is the current timestamp generated by A, to an arabiter called the Central Authority, C. To respond to this request, C executes the following protocol:

```
respond(A*,B*,t);
    A <-- key(A*);
    B <-- key(B*);
    K <-- newkey(t);
    send(A*,E_A(t,B,K,E_B(K,A)).
```

The key K is generated by a key generating procedure for _this session only_, so to insure uniqueness, its definition should depend on the current timestamp. The procedure

```
send(Y,M)
```

simply sends message M to Y over an insecure channel. Thus, after the response from C, A* is the only one who knows the session key, since it has been sent to him under the protection of E_A. That C has responded with t implies that the message is really from C and is not simply being reused by a third party. Finally, the fact that C sends B's name to A guarantees that the intended recipient has not been altered. A then executes

```
send(B*,E_B(K,A).
```

It follows that any future transmissions involving the session key K, must be transmission between A and B, unless the **send** of $(B^*,E_B(K,A))$, instead of originating with A, is simply being replayed to B by a storage channel. One more message exchange is required to convince B that the original **send** is not being mimicked: B must execute

```
t <-- next time stamp
send(A*,E_K(t'));
waitfor(E_K(f(t')),
```

where f is an agreed upon function that does not have to be kept secret.

The public key solution uses both public (P_X) and secret (S_X) keys and the same central authority as before. The exchange is as follows:

A:**request**(A*,B*,E_{P_C}(t))

C:**send**(A*,D_{S_C}(P_B,B))

A:**send**(B*,E_{P_B}(t,A))

B:(t,A) <-- D_{S_B}(E_{P_B}(t,A))
  request(B*,A*,E_{P_C}(t))

C:**send**(B,D_{S_C}(P_A,A)

B:t' <-- next time stamp
  send(A,E_{P_A}(t,t'))

A:**send**(B,E_{P_B}(t')).

The analysis of the public key protocols proceeds in much the same fashion as before. This protocol generalizes to a multiple central authority protocol (in case A and B are mutually suspicious).

4.10 Secure Computer Systems Based on Protocols. We have claimed above that protocols have some significant advantages over software based systems. In this section we will describe protocols and combinations of protocols that can be used to achieve secure computer systems.

4.10.1 Exploiting Technology. Many of the software approaches to secure computer systems depend on a computer technology that is almost fifteen years old. But computer technology has moved considerably beyond such architectures -- particularly in those respects which can most profoundly affect security. The vast bulk of the current crop of operating system security problems arise because of the unrestricted sharing that took place in the computer systems of the 1960's and 1970's. Today, distributed computer systems and advanced communications technology can provide alternative approaches based on protocols. In the following section, we will present a sketch of three computer system organizations which achieve varying levels of security at varying costs. None of these methods depend on technological breakthroughs although all of them depend heavily on the current trend of decreasing hardware costs. The approach we outline below will be fundamentally different from the software oriented approaches in that

1. no software will be trusted to yield the security of the total system, and
2. the security of the total system derives from a few simple hardware devices by easily analyzed arguments.

For simplicity, the bulk of this section is taken up with a discussion of three approaches to the *-property (later we will touch on other security models). The essential properties of these protocols are outlined in the table below.

PROTOCOL	COST	NEED TO TRUST	LEVEL OF SECURITY
A	N^2	simple physics and simple protocols	extremely secure
B	N	simple physics and protocols, encryption and simple logic	requires secure cryptosystems, but can leak a single bit
C	1	simple physics and protocols, encryption, some logic	requires secure cryptosystems, complex protocols that can change accesses in software; still can only leak a single bit

In this table, system cost is measured as a function of the number of security levels, N, to be maintained by the system. Intuitively, the cost is the number of copies of system files, pages or documents to be maintained.

A key piece of hardware required for these systems is the one-way link. This is a device which allows information to flow exclusively in one direction. Confidence in the system is largely limited by confidence in the uni-directional nature of the one-way link. Fiber optic links give an essentially perfect one-way link. (See Figure 4.3). A cannot even tell whether or not B exists, and the only way that B can send information to A is to actually swap the properties of the emitter and sensor. In other words, B must actually convert a light sensing device into a light emitting device. This is a sufficiently blatant act so that we will assume that other monitoring procedures will alert a security manager if the A/B roles are ever reversed.

Figure 4.3
A One-way Optical Link

The 'buffer' in Figure 4.3 is a hardware device to aid in the high-volume transfer of data from A to B; in particular, such a buffer may be needed to insure that timing signals need not be passed from B to A and to avoid redundancy in the transmission.

Assuming such hardware does little good if there are hidden (e.g., software) paths for the information, so we will design a system in which information may only flow between levels over one of these links. As we will discuss later, this does not necessarily imply separate storage for all levels. It does imply that the processing stages of each security level should have no interaction with the processing at any other level. The only way to insure this without trusting any software is to give each level its own computer. The choice of computer is irrelevant for security purposes; the choice is a function of the processing needs at that level and by economic concerns. This is a critical point at which current technology allows solutions which would have been unthinkable five years ago.

4.10.2 Secure Multilevel Systems. For protocol A, we assume

two levels s_1 and s_2. Both levels correspond to an entire computer system. we will complete the design by supplying a way for s_2 to read any of s_1's files and at the same time avoid any information flowing from s_2 to s_1. Assume that both levels use disk storage. Let S_1 be the disk for s_1. There is a 1-way link from S_1 to another disk called the <u>shadow</u> disk for S_1, which will be represented by S_1' (see Figure 4.4)

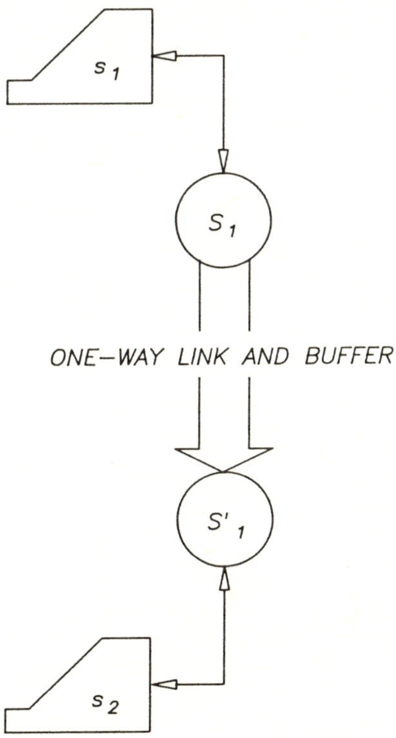

Figure 4.4
Shadow Disk for Security Level s_1

All writes of s_1 to S_1 are sent down the 1-way link to be performed on S_1' as well. At all times, S_1' is a 'shadow' copy of S_1. Whenever s_2 accesses the files of s_1, the access is through

s_1's shadow disk, only.

This protocol offers obvious security. If the 1-way link works, then it is impossible for information to flow from s_2 to s_1.

Two practical problems must be solved. S_1' may lose information during write commands due to rotational delays. This problem can be solved by adjusting performance parameters. A second problem concerns another possible channel which is truly hidden. If S_1' crashes, then the cooperation of S_1 is required to reestablish the disk and to synchronize the disks. Two solutions are possible. First, only synchronize on a planned schedule, independent of all crashes. Second, treat a crash as a compromise of the system, allow it, but report it to the security manager for action. This latter solution figures prominently in later protocols. Note that a compromise of the system is defined to be the possible transmission of information when some externally observable event like a disk crash occurs. Such compromise may well be unavoidable, and a system which is secure except for a compromise in this sense may still be highly useful -- no system is immune from the occurrence of external events and since these events are observable, a manager can be informed when they occur and each event can be investigated individually.

It is easy to construct examples which force protocol A to use $O(N^2)$ disks. Protocol A has another major weakness in that it is difficult to reconfigure the system. The major advantage of the protocol is, of course, its simplicity. It is possible to reduce the cost but such a savings comes at its own price. It will be necessary to rely on more complex hardware and the user must weigh this against the cost of the first approach. There is a tradeoff between what must be trusted in a system and the cost of the system.

To get the basic idea of protocol B, let S_1' be the shadow disk for S_1 as described above. If $s_2, \ldots, s_n$ wish to read any of s_1's files, they can use a queueing strategy to multiplex S_1'. As shown in Figure 4.5, a user in level j can select a record of S_1' and receive it on the read line.

This approach must trust the disk controller (the minimal amount of software which must be trusted in secure kernels). But since we promised protocols which trust no software protocol B must be taken further.

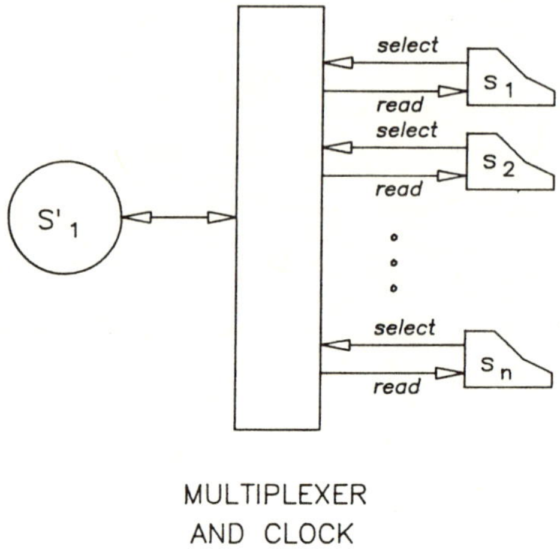

Figure 4.5
Multiplexing The Shadow Disk

By incorporating a time stamp protocol into the multiplexing scheme, it is possible to eliminate reliance on the security of the disk controllers (see Figure 4.6)

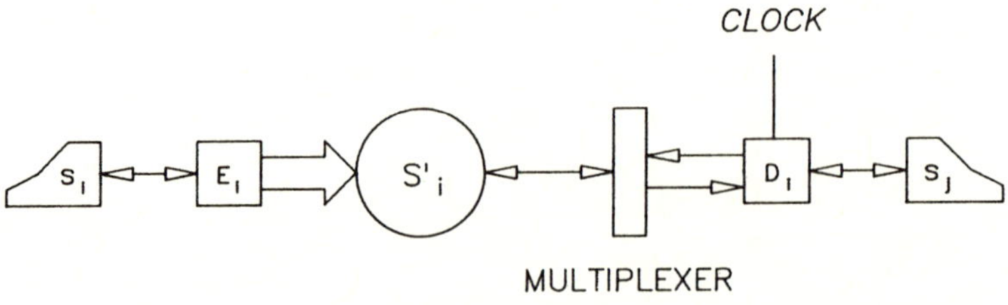

Figure 4.6
Protocol B: Level s_j accessing s_i's shadow disk

The encrypting and decrypting functions may be conventional algorithms such as DES or public key systems. Insofar as these ciphers operate within their known limits of security they may be trusted -- if higher degrees of trust are required, then more highly secure ciphers must be employed. The main operations defined by the protocols are **write** operations to a local disk and **read** operations on a disk belonging to another level. The essential idea here will be the certification of records by means of an encryption operation which couples the record to a time stamp. The encryption key for level i will for the moment be represented by 'i'. $E(i,.)=E_i$ maps a record p and a time stamp t to a mesage q:

$$E_i(p,t) = q.$$

Then clearly,

$$(p,t) = D_i(q),$$

assuming a conventional cipher.

To write p with record key k -- as opposed to a cryptographic key -- a record key is a public name by which the record is known; for example, if p is a page, then k is the page number -- it is only necessary to execute the following protocol:

```
write(p,k);
t<--next time stamp;
q<--E_i(p,t);
send(disk,(k,q));
broadcast over all 1-way links.
```

To read record k from the shadow disk S_i', a level must execute the following protocol:

```
read(k,t);
q<--select(k);
(p',t')<--D_i(q);
if t=t' then return(p') else sound alarm.
```

The protocols simply state that s_i encrypts its record using the round-robin scheduling clock to generate a time stamp, while s_j sends a request to S_i' which it decrypts using key i; if the certificate is incorrect then the request is illegal and an alarm sounds. So to see why these protocols are correct, it is necessary to prove that information cannot flow illegally from s_j to s_i. First, notice that the simple security property allows s_j to know s_i's key i if j is at a higher security level than i. Information can flow to the disk controller. When the controller receives a request, it can fail to respond, but this is an observable event and an alarm can be sounded. If the controller selects the proper record, then there is nothing to be done. If the controller selects any other record, an alarm will sound since the **read** protocol will fail to verify the time stamp. As in the case of A there is a compromise inherent in this protocol, but it is always associated with an external event.

This protocol uses N disks. By adding one more time stamp to the certification procedure, it is possible to reduce this requirement to a single disk for all levels. The **read** protocol is much the same as for protocol B:

> **read**(k,t);
>
> q<--**select**(k);
>
> (p',t',t'')<--D_i(q);
>
> **if** t=t' **then** return(p') **else** sound alarm.

The **write** protocol is more complicated. It is easier to visualize **write** if Figure 4.6 is modified as shown below

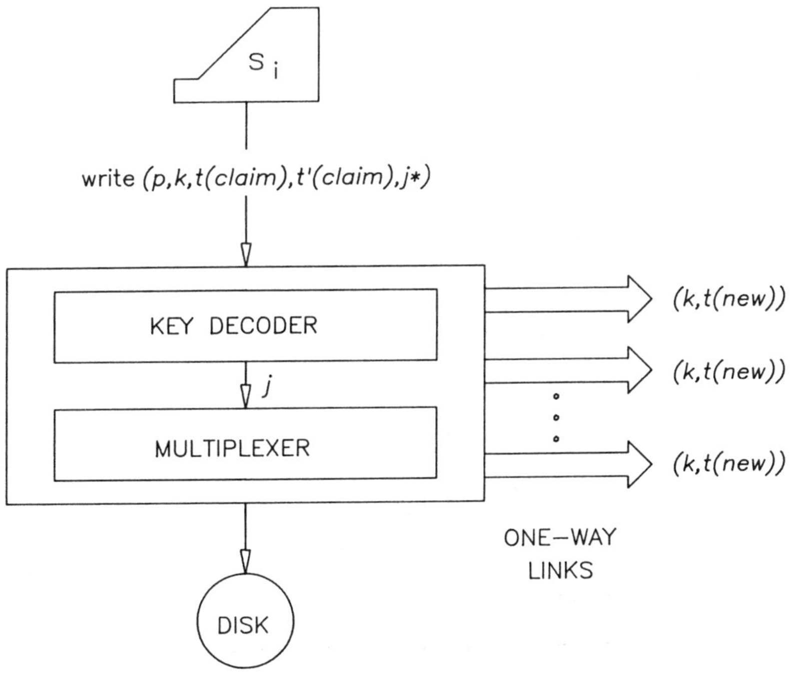

In order for s_i to be able to complete the **write**, he must be able to compose the following list of arguments.

1. p, the record to be written
2. k, the record key,
3. t(claim), the time stamp which i claims will allow page k to be selected.
4. t'(claim), the time stamp which i claims will allow p to be written into the frame retrieved and verified using t(claim).
5. j*, the public name of s_j.

The **write** protocol for C is specified by two protocols **can_write** and **do_write**:

```
can_write(k,t(claim),t'(claim),j*);
j<--D_i(j*);
q<--select(k);
(p(old),t,t')<--D_i(q);
if t = t(claim) and D_j(t')=t'(claim)
      then exit can_write
      else sound alarm;

do_write(k,p);
t(new)<--next time stamp;
q(new)<--E_i(p,t(new),E_j(t(new)));
send(disk,(k,q(new));
broadcast (k,t(new)) over one-way links.
```

4.10.3 More System Functions. The simple protocols above do not yet constitute a computer system. A real computer system must have printers, procedures for downgrading documents, barriers to prevent Trojan horses, etc., and each of these gives rise to new protocols for security. The motivation for each of the protocols is exactly what it was for the *-property protocols.

For example, secure printers can be handled by protocols which combine hardened printers with an authentication protocol. Alternatively, a secure printer may be handled through a central authority.

Selective downgrading of documents requires a central authority. If the principle security property is the *-property, then every downgrading of a document is an explicit security violation. There is apparently no way to avoid the use of an arbiter to authorize the downgrading of documents. The main problems to be addressed in such a protocol are the authorization problem, the integrity problem and the problem of flagging the request to a manager with a means of auditing the transactions. Such a protocol works as follows. Suppose s_j requests the downgrading of a document from level s_k to level s_i. The request is processed through an arbiter who authorizes the request. This is an authorization problem which is much like those dealt with above. When the command has been authorized, the arbiter places a request to s_k to show the document to be downgraded. Level s_k then retrieves the requested record and shows it to the arbiter. If the arbiter approves, he requires s_k to digitally sign the record to prove that s_k has retrieved the proper record, then signs the record himself to prevent s_k from substituting another record for the actual transmission to s_i. The arbiter then conducts an exchange of session keys between s_k and s_i and requests level s_k to transmit to level s_i through an unprotected channel. The arbiter notes the transmission as a violation of the *-property. When level s_i receives the document, its access hardware writes it to its disk as in the previous section after verifying that the signatures affixed by s_k and by the arbiter are correct. As before, alarms are rung if there is a violation at any stage of the process.

As a final example, consider the protocols necessary to insure that the confinement property is satisfied. The key issue is the one of making certain that programs only execute within their authorized domains. For example, by using hardware devices to access privileged mode programs, an operating system can be prevented from executing any privileged mode program that has not been properly signed. Such a protocol would check the signatures of privileged programs each time they are loaded into memory. Carried to its conclusion, such a protocol would require a hardware device to be inserted into the computer's instruction fetch-execute cycle to decipher program instructions. Without a proper key, it would be physically impossible for a program to operate outside its intended environment simply because the instructions would be scrambled.

4.11 Compromising Protocols. The security of any system is, of course, dependent upon the resources and capabilities available to an attacker. The security provided by particular cryptographic transformations has traditionally been measured by the difficulty of ciphertext-only, plaintext-ciphertext, and chosen plaintext attacks.

The first two attacks correspond to a situation in which an attacker can "eavesdrop" on some system activity, while the third usually involves an additional ability to selectively interact with the system. Attacks may thus be classified as _active_ or _passive_. A passive attack is one in which the attacker is limited to observing the activity of certain system components as by eavesdropping on communication channels. An active attacker is one who selectively alters the state of system components: introducing, deleting or altering messages on a channel, destroying a channel or computer installation, or altering stored information are all examples of active attacks.

Passive attacks are solely concerned with obtaining specific information about the system -- they attempt to combine cryptanalysis of specific messages with inferences from observed system activity to obtain the information required. The analysis of channel activity, with little or no concern for the contents of encrypted messages, is called _traffic analysis_. Passive attacks may be aimed at obtaining information permitting a successful and more serious active attack -- by obtaining an access code for a particular restricted resource, for instance.

Active attacks may have more diverse objectives. They may be aimed at obtaining information or unauthorized use of other resources, degrading performance (_denial of service_ attacks), or corrupting stored information. A resourceful attacker may opportunistically carry out any or all of these operations!

Active attacks pose a particular hazard in systems of <u>mutually suspicious</u> components, in which the attacker may be a legitimate user or group of users of the system. Such systems must strike a careful balance between providing sufficient capability to allow each potential attacker to function correctly and preventing subversion of system security. The key distribution and mental poker protocols are examples of protocols designed for such applications.

Attacks on protocols arise from many system weaknesses. The physical environment of the protocol is often enough to invalidate it. On the other hand, the environment may be adequately secure, but the underlying cryptosystem may be flawed. Finally, even in a secure environment, with a secure cryptosystem, the logic of the protocol may lead to compromise.

Perhaps the simplest of all protocols is secure message transmission. Suppose A wants to send a secret message to B using a public key system. A looks up B's public key in a directory of public keys and sends $E(P_A,(M)$ to B. This is a secure transmission if the public key functions are secure, <u>and</u> if the directory has not be compromised. For suppose that a third party, C, has modified A's directory by substituting his public key for B's. Then when A sends his message to B, C can read it, but B cannot.

Other very simple protocols have similarly obvious flaws. Consider, for instance, using a public key system to sign messages. A signs a message, M, by decrypting it with his secret key to obtain a signed message $D(S_A,M)$. If A then sends $D(S_A,M)$ to B, he can encrypt it with A's public key. Since only A knows his S_A

key, it is impossible to forge his signature. Furthermore, since B can recover M, it is not possible to change the contents of a signed document. However, A can cheat. By _publishing_ his secret key, A can claim that his signature has been compromised and thus successfully disavow any document signed using that key.

Often, the existence of an attack suggests improvements in the underlying protocol. Consider the following application of a public key system. We assume that an enemy cannot substitute his own public key for another user's. If A receives public key P from B, A can secretly communicate with B. There is no authentication in this protocol, however, since _anyone_ can impersonate A by sending $E(P_B,M)$. If E, D satisfy

$$M = E_K(D_{K'}(M))$$

for all M, then the system can be used for both signatures and secrecy. The following protocol provides secret, signed communication with receipts between A and B. Using the notation of 4.9, A executes **send**$(B, E(P_B,D(S_A,M)))$. Upon receipt B recovers $D(S_A,M)$ and hence M. Finally, B executes **send**$(A,E(P_A,D(S_B,M)))$ to provide a notice of receipt.

However, without cryptanalysis, this protocol can be compromised. The enemy, C, records $x = E(P_A,D(S_B,M))$ and sends x to A identifying x as _his_ message. Since A believes $x = E(P_A,D(S_C\cdot y)))$ for some y, A forms $E(P_C,D(S_A,x))) = E(P_C,D(S_B,M))$. If A now responds by executing

send$(C,E(P_C,D(S_A,E(P_C,D(S_B,M))))),$

M can easily be recovered.

The mental poker protocol described above is secure. That is, the process of locking and unlocking boxes yields a secure protocol, if the locks are strong enough. The locks described in the implementation are apparently as strong as any public key cryptosystem.

Still, it is possible to cheat undetectably in this implementation. If M is a perfect square modulo n, then so is $E_K(M)$. Thus, the encryption function <u>preserves quadratic residues</u>. It is, therefore, possible to cheat without actually breaking the underlying cryptosystem. A player simply uses the fact that a card is a quadratic residue as a "mark" on the card. This does not reveal much about the hands, but in a game of poker, even a bit of information about the cards dealt can be an advantage in the long run.

These examples illustrate protocol-based attacks on the underlying cryptosystem. Such attacks can be used to compromise the crypto-security of ciphers when applied to the basic communication protocols. It is important to note that none of these attacks subvert the complexity based separation of encrypting and decrypting keys (e.g., the attacks do not follow factoring of a public key n = pq).

Suppose that a message $M = (m_1, \ldots, m_k)$ is encrypted with a knapsack using public key $(a_1, \ldots, a_k) = K$:

$$E(K,M) = S = \sum_{i=1}^{k} a_i m_i$$

If the communication protocol broadcasts $E(K_j,M)$ to d recipients for large d, then it is possible to solve for M without solving a knapsack. Suppose $d = k$ and consider the $k \times k$ matrix

$$A = \begin{bmatrix} a_{11} & a_{12} \cdots & a_{1k} \\ a_{21} & a_{22} \cdots & a_{2k} \\ \vdots & \vdots & \vdots \\ a_{k1} & a_{k2} \cdots & a_{kk} \end{bmatrix}$$

where for each $1 \leq i \leq k$ $(a_{i1},\ldots,a_{ik})$ is the public key K_i. Then each K_i enciphers M : $E(K_i,M) = s_i$, so that

$$s = \begin{bmatrix} s_1 \\ \vdots \\ s_k \end{bmatrix} = A \cdot (m_1,\ldots,m_k)^T$$

In general, A will be nonsingular so it is possible to solve for M:

$$M = A^{-1} \cdot s$$

Thus, given a broadcast communication protocol, there is a ciphertext-only cryptanalysis of a knapsack cipher. Since knapsacks are already compromised by Shamir's algorithm, this attack is of only theoretical importance. Howeever, other public key cryptosystems can be compromised by protocol-based attacks which are similar in spirit to the ciphertext-only attack given above.

For notational convenience, we represent the encryption and decryption transformations determined by a pair of keys P_A, S_A as follows:

$$E(M) = E(P_A,M)$$

$$D(M) = E(S_A, M)$$

Given an example of ciphertext E(M), a cryptanalyst wants to solve for M. The line of attack is to use the ciphertext and signatures of messages x, D(x), obtained from the holder of the secret key to obtain a set of values E(M),D(x),D(y),... . If these values are algebraically related in the sense that for some algebraic (in the ring of integers which represent plaintext messages) function G,

$$G(M,E(M),D(x),D(y),\ldots) = 0,$$

then the cryptanalyst can solve for M. In general, this requires that E and D be algebraic over the plaintext messages. Suppose, for example, that messages are chosen from the integers mod n, Z_n, and that D is a multiplication automorphism of Z_n: $D(xy) = D(x) \cdot D(y)$ for $x,y \in Z_n$. Then, given E(M), a cryptanalyst can obtain signatures on an arbitrary $x \in Z_n$. In particular $D(x \cdot E(M))$ can be obtained. Since x can be chosen so that $(D(x),n) = 1$ and the cryptanalyst can form

$$(D(x))^{-1} D(x \cdot E(M)) = D(x)^{-1} D(x) D(E(M)) = M.$$

By a similar argument, it is possible to force an arbitrary signature on the holder of the secret key for D: Choose a message M to be signed and form

$$D(x)^{-1}\ D(x \cdot M) = D(M).$$

All of the public key algorithms described previously succumb to this style of attack

<u>RSA</u>: Let

$$E(M) = M^e \bmod n$$

$$D(M) = M^d \bmod n.$$

Clearly $D(xy) = (xy)^d = x^d y^d \bmod n.$

<u>Rabin's Quadratic Scheme</u>: Using the 4-1 encryption scheme

$$E(M) = M^2 \bmod n$$

$$D(M) = M^{1/2} \bmod n,$$

we obtain

$$D(x)^{-1} D(x \cdot E(M)) = x^{-1/2}[x \cdot E(M)]^{1/2} = E(M)^{1/2} = M.$$

<u>Encryption in Ring of Algebraic Numbers</u>: Recall that

$$E(x,y) = \underbrace{(x,y) \cdot (x,y) \cdot \ \dots \ \cdot (x,y)}_{e \text{ times}}$$

$$D(x,y) = \underbrace{(x,y) \cdot (x,y) \cdot \ \dots \ \cdot (x,y)}_{d \text{ times}}$$

where multiplication is the pointwise defined multiplication in $Q(\sqrt{s})$ for square-free s.

To recover (M_1, M_2) from $E(M_1, M_2) = (C_1, C_2)$, obtain a signature $D(x_1C_1, x_2C_2)$ for arbitrary message (x_1, x_2). Let u, v be solutions to

$$C_1 = ux_1C_1 + svx_2C_2 \bmod n$$

$$C_2 = ux_2C_2 + vx_1C_1$$

Multiplication in $Q(\sqrt{s})$ is both commutative and associative so

$$(u,v)\cdot(x_1C_1, x_2C_2) = (C_1, C_2).$$

Hence

$$D(u,v)D(x_1C_1, x_2C_2) = \underbrace{(C_1, C_2) \cdot (C_1,C_2)\ldots(C_1,C_2)}_{d \text{ times}}$$

A slight variant of the attack also compromises a signature knapsack. Knapsacks, in general, are not automorphisms of Z_n, but the protocol for signature knapsacks require a validation test TEST(M,C) to determine whether or not

$$C \dot{A} = M \bmod n$$

where A is the private key used to form D(M).

Obtaining D(x) and D(xM) requires obtaining X, Y such that

$$XA = x \bmod n \text{ and } YA = x+M \bmod n.$$

Notice that

$$(Y-X)A = YA - XAx + M-x = M \bmod n.$$

But then TEST(Y-X,M) is true and a signature has been forged that will pass adjudication. Since the signature function itself actually produces one signature from a <u>set</u> of signatures which pass TEST, Y-X may not be the signature which the holder of A would have actually produced, but TEST does not require that.

The effects of this attack can be limited in practical situations by modifying the signature protocols.

4.12 Establishing Protocol Security. We have seen protocols which are apparently secure, yet have been subjected to successful attacks. Not only is it difficult to design and implement secure protocols, it is evidently difficult to analyze the properties of protocols.

The classical analyses of cryptographic properties which stem from Shannon's information theoretic model of security, provide for absolute security. According to this approach, ciphertext provides secrecy if an attacker with unlimited resources could do no better than guess the associated cleartext from among all possible cleartexts of that length. The fewer cleartexts among which the attacker must guess, the less secrecy the encryption technique provides. One result of this definition of secrecy is that the space of cryptographic keys must be as large as the space of cleartexts -- since an attacker can guess keys as well as cleartexts. Absolutely secure encryption techniques thus require the key to be essentially as large as the total amount of text it is used to encrypt. However useful the theory, it is generally believed to be far too pessimistic -- many useful encipherment techniques (e.g., public-key systems and DES) are not secure in the information theoretic model.

The private key in public-key systems, for instance, is completely determined by the value of the public key. On the other hand, it is hidden by a particularly difficult computation, and in practice an attacker will not have unlimited computing resources at his disposal. Secrecy and other security properties of modern cryptographic systems rest on an attacker's practical limitations; he must either guess a value from an impossibly large set, or complete an impossibly lengthy computation. Unfortunately, proofs of the difficulty of performing particular classes of computations, particularly those of importance to cryptography, have eluded researchers. Practical modern cryptography therefore depends upon the _belief_ that particular computations, such as factorization, are difficult. Support for this belief rests on the resistance of such problems to years of analysis.

Since protocol security rests on the security of underlying cryptographic transformations, rigorous analysis of protocol security must suffer the same limitations. The best that can be hoped for is a demonstration of security that meets contemporary standards of mathematical rigor. Such a result will assert that _either_ the protocol is secure _or_ that some explicit cryptographic assumption of the difficulty of a problem is wrong.

The insecure protocols mentioned above succumb to two different weaknesses. The poker protocol falls to an attack on a cryptographic property necessary to the protocol, but not made explicit by the designers (namely, that cards cannot be marked). Other protocols on the other hand, have serious logical weaknesses that no purely cryptographic strengthening can correct: the power of the cryptosystem needed to implement the protocol provides an attacker with the very tools he needs to force an old key on a user.

A careful protocol designer should thus perform a two-step verification of a protocol's security:

1. identify explicit cryptographic assumptions

2. determine that any successful attack on the protocol <u>requires</u> the violation of at least one assumption made in step 1.

The best form for step 2 to take would be a proof capable of convincing a knowledgeable reader.

This two-step method has occasionally been followed in careful presentations of a few secure protocols. A recent example is a secure mental poker protocol. This protocol exploits the oblivious transfer and other number-theoretic tools; the designers prove that obtaining <u>any</u> information about an opponent's hand violates an explicit cryptographic assumption.

More general techniques for exploring the security properties of classes of protocols are being explored. In public-key systems, or in private-key systems in which some keys may be compromised, an attacker is assumed to have certain limited cryptographic capabilities. The capabilities may be exploited in active attacks that permit the attacker to make inferences about the rest of the system -- and to successfully violate security requirements.

The key to such an approach is the creation of an abstract, axiomatically secure system of cryptographic transformations and predicates that reflects the general properties of the actual cryptosystems utilized by the protocol. The following example illustrates how this may be accomplished.

We will model a simple public-key system for two users, A and B. Let M be the set of all possible messages, and $C = \{c_1, c_2, \ldots\}$

be a subset of M, the cleartext messages. The elements of C may be English sentences, or may contain particular redundancy information, but we assume that both A and B can determine whether a message is cleartext or not. The public key encryption functions are mappings between messages, $e_A, e_B: M \rightarrow M$. In this example, we expect e_A and e_B (encryption with A or B's public key, respectively) to satisfy certain properties, for all messages n and m:

1. No fixed points; $e_A(m) \neq m$,

2. Disjoint ranges; $e_A(m) \neq e_B(n)$,

3. Ranges and C disjoint; $e_A(m), e_B \notin C$.

It is worth noting that actual public key encryption functions seldom have disjoint ranges (property 2). However, protocol designers may assume that finding two messages m and n such that $e_A(m) = e_B(n)$ is an intractable problem. This cryptographic assumption becomes an explicit axiom of our abstract cryptosystem.

The decryption functions, e_A^{-1} and e_B^{-1}, are partial functions inverting e_A and e_B, respectively. Here we assume that messages can be decrypted with a secret key only if they are encryptions of some other message, with the associated public key. In practice, this may be accomplished by appending some redundant information before encrypting a message. Thus, A can learn if some message has been encrypted with his public key, by inverting the encryption and detecting the redundancy. A's ability to draw such inferences about messages is described by a predicate E_A; $E_A(x)$ is true if and only if $x = e_A(y)$ for some message y. B has a similar predicate E_B. From property 2 of the encryption function, $E_A(x)$

implies $\neg E_B(x)$.

The set M, subset C, predicates E_A and E_B and functions e_A, e_B e_A^{-1} and e_B^{-1} are an abstract public-key cryptosystem. Assuming they have exchanged public keys, A and B have a well-defined set of cryptographic capabilities. Other than by receiving messages, these capabilities are the only ways in which B or A can learn new messages or make inferences about the cryptosystem.

Now suppose A has acquired only three messages; $c_A, e_B(c_A)$ and $e_B(c_B)$. Even though A cannot decrypt $e_B(c_A)$ directly, he can apply e_B to c_A and compare the result with $e_B(c_A)$, identifying that message. But about $e_B(c_B)$, A knows much less -- A knows it is not cleartext, is not an encryption with his public key, i.e., $\neg E_A(e_{B_k}(c_B))$, and is not a multiple encryption of c_A with B's public key $(e_B(c_A)) \neq e_B(c_B)$, for any $k > 0$). Indeed, so far as A can tell. $e_B(c_B)$ could be the encryption using e_B of <u>any</u> message m in M not available to him. A's ignorance has a formal analog -- it is possible to define a consistent renaming of all the messages in M that exchanges c_B and m. This renaming defines a new cryptosystem, in which $e_B(c_B)$ is the encryption with B's public key of the message m. Since the renaming preserves the structure of the original cryptosystem, it is called an <u>automorphism</u>. There are two crucial properties to this particular automorphism: decrypting $e_B(c_B)$ in the renamed system yields m, and the automorphism is <u>hidden</u> from A: the part of the cryptosystem of which A has knowledge remains unaffected by the renaming. In this example, the automorphism is $\xi: M \to M$, where

$$\xi(c_B) = m,$$

$$\xi(m) = c_B,$$

and

$$\xi(n) = n, \text{ for } c_B \neq n \neq m.$$

Since $\xi(n)$ for all n to which n has access, the automorphism is hidden from A. Furthermore, closing all relations and functions under ξ gives an isomorphic cryptosystem so that any attack that A mounts will also be an an attack on the isomorphic system. In short, given A's capabilities and currently available information, there is no local experiment he can perform to determine which of the original or renamed system is correct. Both are consistent extensions of his current knowledge.

The algebraic structures used to define these abstract cryptosystems models the encryption-decryption process by operations on sets of strings. Specifically, if $C = \{c_1, \ldots, c_k\}$ and $B = \{e_1, \ldots, e_j\}$ are disjoint sets of symbols, then the application of the encryption function e_i to cleartext c is given by $e_i(c) = e_i c$. Thus, the set of messages that can be constructed in the cryptosystem is $M = B^*C$. By the same token, $e^{-1}_i(x\omega) = \omega$, if $x = e_i$. Additional structure models more complex constructions such as commutative functions and random protocols.

4.13 Bibliographic Notes. The Lucifer System is described in [32]. A good survey of signature schemes is [55]. The proposal to use public key schemes for signatures is due to Diffie and Hellman [27]. The use of the RSA algorithm is explicit in [70]. Rabin's algorithm was first presented in [68] and has since been refined several times. Shamir [73] has considered the problem of speeding up the signature process. The application of the quadratic encryption function to signatures is described by Rabin [67].

Mental Poker was proposed in [78] and the scheme for cheating is due to Lipton [52]. Many of the remaining protocols are due to Merkle [57]. The key sharing protocol based on interpolation presented here is due to Shamir [78], while the scheme based on algebraic coding theory was proposed by Davida, DeMillo, and Lipton [11]. [81] presents another authorization protocol. The ability to carry out authenticated communication in a distributed system was demonstrated by Needham and Schroeder [62].

Oblivious transfers were invented by Rabin to solve a problem posed by DeMillo. An account of the oblivious transfer is given by Blum [6]; see also the survey paper by DeMillo and Merritt [22] for applications. The protocol for secret ballot elections appeared in Merritt's thesis [59] and also appears in [20] along with a hidden automorphsim proof of security. The protocol for password protection by iterating one-way functions is due to Lamport [48].

Schemes for attacks on protocols include the broadcast attack on knapsacks due to Miller [60], the authentication compromise, due to Dolev and Yao [30] and the chosen signature attack, due to Davida [10,21].

The algebraic approach to establishing the security of protocols was first considered by Dolev and Yao. Merritt, DeMillo and Lynch [20] generalized the structure and defined hidden automorphisms. Merritt's thesis contains several applications of hidden automorphism models to complex protocols [59].

The suggestion that technology can be employed to replace kernelized approaches has been 'in the wind' for some time [42], but the first such protocols are due to Davida, DeMillo and Lipton [12]. Using protocols to confine programs was also suggested by Merkle [57].

5. Bibliography

[1] A. Aho, J. Hopcroft and J. Ullman, 'The Design and Analysis of Computer Algorithms,' Addison- Wesley, 1974.

[2] D. Bell and L. LaPadula, 'Secure Computer Systems: Mathematical Foundations and Model,' MITRE Report, MTR-2547, volume 2, November 1973.

[3] E. R. Berlekamp, 'Factoring Polynomials over Large Finite Fields,' Mathematics of Computation, volume 24, (1978), pp. 713-735.

[4] Bishop, M. and Snyder, L., 'The Transfer of Information and Authority in a Protection System', Proceedings of the Seventh Symposium on Operating System Principles, 1979.

[5] R. Blakely and G. Blakely, 'Security of Number Theoretic Public Key Cryptosystems Against Random Attack I,II,III' Cryptologia, to appear.

[6] M. Blum, 'How to Exchange Secret Keys', University of California, Berkeley, UCB/ERLM81/90, March, 1982.

[7] G. Brassard, S. Fortune and J. Hopcroft, 'A Note on Crypotgraphy and NP co-NP,' TR 78-338, Department of Computer Science, Cornell University, 1978.

[8] Budd, T. and Lipton, R.J., 'On Classes of Protection Systems', in DeMillo, R.A. et al (editors) Foundations of Secure Computation, Academic Press, Inc. New York, 1978.

[9] Cohen, Ellis S., Problems, Mechanisms and Solutions PhD Dissertation, Carnegie-Mellon University, 1976.

[10] George I. Davida, 'Chosen Signature Cryptanalysis of the RSA (MIT) Public Key Cryptosystem,' unpublished manuscript.

[11] G. Davida, R. DeMillo, and R. Lipton, 'Sharing Cryptographic Keys,' IEEE Symposium on Security and Privacy, Berkeley, CA, April 1980.

[12] G. Davida, R. DeMillo and R. Lipton, 'A System Architecture to Support a Verifiably Secure Multilevel Security System,' IEEE Symposium on Security and Privacy, Berkeley, CA, April 1980.

[13] G. Davida and J. Kam, 'A Structured Design of Substitution-Permutation Encryption Networks,' in DeMillo, R. A. et al (editors), Foundations of Secure Computation, Academic Press, 1978, pp. 95-114.

[14] R. DeMillo, 'Database Security,' Issues in Database Management, edited by H. Weber and A. Wasserman, North-Holland, 1979, pp. 253- 256.

[15] R. DeMillo and D. Dobkin, 'Recent Progress in Secure Computation,'1978 IEEE Compsac Conference, Chicago, IL, November 1978.

[16] R. DeMillo, D. Dobkin and R. Lipton, 'Even Databases That Lie Can be Compromised,' IEEE Transactions on Software Engineering, volume SE-4, number 1, (January, 1978), pp. 73-75.

[17] R. DeMillo, D. Dobkin and R. Lipton, 'Combinatorial Inference,' in DeMillo, R.A. et al (editors), Foundations of Secure Computation, Academic Press, 1978, p 27-38.

[18] R. DeMillo, R. Lipton and A. Perlis, 'Social Processes and Proofs of Theorems and Programs,' Communications of the ACM, volume 22, number 5, (May, 1979), pp. 272-280.

[19] R. DeMillo, D. Dobkin, R. Lipton and A. Jones, Foundations of Secure Computation, Academic Press, 1978.

[20] R. A. DeMillo, N. A. Lynch and M. J. Merritt, 'Cryptographic Protocols,' Proceedings 14th ACM Symposium on Theory of Computing, May 1982, 383-400.

[21] R. A. DeMillo and M. J. Merritt, 'Chosen Signature Cryptanalysis of Public Key Cryptosystems,' Technical Memorandum, School of Information and Computer Science, Georgia Institute of Technology, Atlanta, GA, October,1982.

[22] R. A. DeMillo and M. J. Merritt, 'Protocols for Data Security,' Computer, volume 16, number 2, February, 1983, pp. 39-50.

[23] C. A. Deavours, 'How the British Broke Enigma,' Cryptologia, volume 4, number 3 (July, 1980), pp. 1219-132.

[24] D. Denning and P. Denning, 'Data Security', Computing Surveys, September 1979, pp. 227-250.

[25] D. E. Denning, P. J. Denning, S. J. Garland, M. A. Harrison, and W. L. Ruzzo, 'Proving Protection Systems Safe', unpublished manuscript, 1977.

[26] B. DeWolf and P. Szulewski, editors, 'Final Report of the 1979 Summer Study on AirForce Computer Security,' Draper Labs Report R-1326, October, 1979.

[27] W. Diffie and M. Hellman, 'New Directions in Cryptogaphy,' IEEE Transactions on Information Theory, volume IT-22, number 6, (November, 1976), pp. 644-654.

[28] W. Diffie and M. Hellman, 'Exhaustive Cryptanalysis of the NBS Data Encryption Standard,' Computer, volume 10, number 6 (June, 1977), pp. 74-84.

[29] D. Dobkin, A. Jones and R. Lipton, 'Secure Data Bases: Protection Against User Inference,' ACM Transactions on Database Systems, volume 4, number 1, (March, 1979) pp. 97-106.

[30] D. Dolev and A. Yao, 'On the Security of Public Key Protocols,' Proceedings 22nd Annual FOCS Symposium, IEEE, October, 1981, pp. 350-357.

[31] S. Even and Y. Yacobi, 'Cryptocomplexity and NP Completeness,' (unpublished manuscript).

[32] H. Feistel, 'Cryptography and Computer Privacy,' Scientific American, volume 228 (May, 1973), pp. 15-23.

[33] Ford Aerospace, 'Secure Minicomputer Operating System KSOS: Computer Program Development Specifications, Type B-5, Department of Defense Kernelized Secure Operating System. I. Security Kernel, II. Unix Emulator, III. Security Related Software, Report WDL-TR7811, July 1978.

[34] Martin Gardner, Mathematical Games, Scientific American, volume 237, (August, 1977), pp. 120-124.

[35] Harrison, M.A., <u>Introduction to Formal Language Theory</u>, Addison-Wesley, Reading, Mass, 1978. 461-471.

[36] Harrison, M.A. and Ruzzo, W.L., 'Monotonic Protection Systems', in DeMillo, R.A. et al (editors) <u>Foundations of Secure Computation</u>, Academic Press, Inc., New York, 1978.

[37] M. Harrison, W. Ruzzo and J. Ullman, 'Protection in Operating Systems,' Communications of the ACM, volume 19, (1976), pp. 461-471.

[38] Martin E. Hellman, 'An Extension of the Shannon Theory Approach to Cryptography,' IEEE Trans. on Information Theory, volume IT-23 (May, 1977), pp. 289-294.

[39] Martin E. Hellman, 'An Overview of Public Key Cryptography,' IEEE Trans. on Communications, volume COM-16, (November, 1978), pp. 24-32.

[40] Martin E. Hellman, 'The Mathematics of Public Key Cryptography,' Scientific American, volume 241 (August, 1979), pp. 146-157.

[41] T. Herlestrom, 'Critical Remarks on Some Public-Key Cryptosystems,' BIT, volume 18, (1978), pp. 493-496.

[42] Bruce Hoard, 'Technology Advances Seen Outpacing Security,' Computer World, June 23,1980,p. 15.

[43] Jones, Anita, K., Protection in Programmed Systems PhD Dissertation, Carnegie-Mellon University, 1973.

[44] A. Jones, R. Lipton and L. Snyder, 'A Linear Time Algorithm for Deciding Security,' 17th IEEE FOCS Conference, Houston, TX, October, 1976.

[45] David Kahn, The Codebreakers: The Story of Secret Writing, MacMillan, New York, 1967.

[46] R.M. Karp, 'Reducibility Among Combinatorial Problems,' Complexity of Computer Computations, in Miller, R. and Thatcher, J, editors, Plenum Press, New York, 1972, pp. 85-104.

[47] S. Kullback, Statistical Methods in Cryptanalysis, NSA Technical Monograph Series, Aegean Park Press, Laguna Hill, CA, 1976.

[48] L. Lamport, Password Authentication with Insecure Communication,' Communications of the ACM, volume 24, number 11, (Novermber, 1981), pp. 770-772.

[49] Lampson, Butler W., 'Protection', Proceedings of the Fifth Princeton Conference on Information Science and Systems, 437-443, 1971.

[50] B. Lampson, 'A Note on the Confinement Problem,' Communications of the ACM, volume 16, numbr 10, (October, 1973), pp. 613-615.

[51] R.J.Lipton, 'An Improved Power Encryption Method,' unpublished manuscript, 1981.

[52] R. J. Lipton, 'How to Cheat at Mental Poker,' unpublished manuscript, 1980

[53] R. J. Lipton, 'A Public Key Encryption Method Based on Algebraic Number Theory,' unpublished manuscript, 1981.

[54] R. Lipton and L.Snyder, 'A Linear Time Algorithm for Deciding Subject Security,' Journal of the ACM, volume 24,number 3, (July, 19779), pp.

[55] S. Matyas, 'Digital Signatures -- An Overview' Computer Networks, volume 3 (1979), pp87-94.

[56] Ralph Merkle, 'Secure Communications over Insecure Channels,' Communications of the ACM, volume 21, number 4 (April, 1978), pp. 294-299.

[57] Ralph Merkle, 'Protocols Based on Public Key Systems,' 1980 IEEE Symposium on Security and Privacy, April, 1980, Berkeley, CA.

[58] Ralph Merkle and Martin Hellman, 'Hiding Information Trapdoor Knapsacks,' IEEE Transactions on Information Theory, volume IT-24, number 5 (September, 1978), pp. 525-530.

[59] M. J. Merritt, Cryptographic Protocols, Ph. D. Thesis, Georgia Institue of Technology, Atlanta, GA, (also appears as report GIT-ICS-83/06, February, 1983).

[60] Donald V. Miller, 'Ciphertext Only Attack on the Merkle-Hellman Public-Key System Under Broadcast Situations,' Cryptologia, volume 6, number 3, (July, 1982), pp. 279-281.

[61] National Bureau of Standards, 'Data Encryption Standard,' FIPS PUB 46, JAnuary 15, 1977

[62] Roger Needham and Michael Schroeder, 'Using Encryption for Authentication in Large Networks of Computers,' Communications of the ACM, volume 21, number 12 (December, 1978) pp. 993-999.

[63] Peter Neumann, Richard Fiertag, Karl Levitt and L Robinson, 'Software Development and Proofs of Multilevel Security,' 1976 Software Engineering Conference, pp. 421-428

[64] D. Parker, _Crime by Computer_, Scribners, New York, 1976.

[65] G. Popek and C. Kline, 'Encryption Protocols, Public-Key Algorithms and Digital Signatures in Computer Networks, ' in DeMillo, R.A. et al (editors), _Foundations of Secure Computation_, Academic Press, 1978, pp. 133-154.

[66] Post, E.L., 'A Variant of a Recursively Unsolvable Problem', Bulletin of the American Mathematical Society 264-268, 1946.

[67] M. O. Rabin, 'Digitalized Signatures and Public- Key Functions as Intractable as Factorization,' MIT Report MIT/LCS/TR-212, January, 1979.

[68] M. O. Rabin, 'Digitalized Signatures,' in DeMillo, R.A. et al (editors), _Foundations of Secure Computation_, Academic Press, 1978, pp. 155-170.

[69] S. Reiss, 'A Combinatorial Model of Database Security,' Journal of the ACM, voume, 25, number 4, (October, 19789, pp.

[70] R. Rivest, A. Shamir and L. Adelman, 'A Method for Obtaining Digital Signatures and Public-Key Cryptosystems,' Communications of the ACM, volume 21, number 2 (February, 1978), pp. 120-126.

[71] Rogers, H. Jr., _Theory of Recursive Functions and Effective Computability_, Mc-Graw-Hill Book Company, New York, 1967.

[72] Jerome Saltzer and Michael Schroeder, 'Protection of Information in Computer Systems,' Proceedings of the IEEE, 1975.

[73] A. Shamir, 'A Fast Signature Scheme,' MIT Report MIT/LCS/TM-107.

[74] A. Shamir, 'On the Cryptocomplexity of Knapsacks,' MIT Report MIT/LCS/TM-129, April 1979.

[75] A. Shamir, 'How to Share A Secret,' MIT Report MIT/LCS/TM-134, May 1979.

[76] A. Shamir, 'The Cryptographic Complexity of Compact Knapsacks,' MIT Report MIT/LCS/TM-164, April 1980.

[77] A. Shamir, 'A Polynoial Time Algorithm for Breaking the Merkle-Hellman Cryptosystem,' (abstract, 1982).

[78] A. Shamir, R.Rivest and L. Adelman, 'Mental Poker' MIT Report MIT/LCS/TM-125, February, 1979.

[79] A. Shamir and R.E. Sippel, 'On the Security of the Merkel-Hellman Cryptographic Scheme,' MIT Report MIT/LCS/TM-119, December, 1978.

[80] C.E. Shannon, 'Communication Theory of Secrecy Systems,' Bell System Tech. Journal, volume 28 (October, 19499, pp. 656-715.

[81] G. Simmons, 'Symmetric and Asymmetric Encryption,' Computing Surveys, volume 11, (December, 1979) 305-330.

[82] G. Simmons, 'Secure Communications in the Presence of Pervasive Deceit,' 1980 IEEE Symposium on Security and Privacy, Berkeley, CA, April 1980.

[83] A. Sinkov, Elementary Cryptanalysi: A Mathematical Approach, Mathematical Association of America, 1966.

[84] Snyder, L., 'Formal Models of Capability-Based Protection Systems', IEEE Transactions on Computers, C-30, 172-181, 1981.

[85] Herbert O. Yardley, The American Black Chamber. Bobbs-Merrill Publishers, Indianapolis, 1931.

ABCDEFGHIJ–CM–89876543